THE
STEPHEN
KING
ILLUSTRATED COMPANION

THE
STEPHEN
KING
ILLUSTRATED COMPANION

MANUSCRIPTS, CORRESPONDENCE, DRAWINGS, AND MEMORABILIA
FROM THE MASTER OF MODERN HORROR

by BEV VINCENT

METRO BOOKS
NEW YORK

FOR MARY ANNE

This 2009 edition published by Metro Books,
by arrangement with becker&mayer! LLC.

The Stephen King Illustrated Companion is produced by
becker&mayer!, Bellevue, Washington.
www.beckermayer.com

Design by Kasey Free and Joanna Price
Editorial by Meghan Cleary
Photo Research by Chris Campbell
Production Coordination by Tom Miller

Metro Books
122 Fifth Avenue
New York, NY 10011

ISBN: 978-1-4351-1766-2

Printed and bound in China

10 9 8 7 6 5 4 3 2

CONTENTS

INTRODUCTION
MR. HORROR U.S.A.

"WHATEVER HAPPENS TO US FEEDS INTO WHATEVER WE WRITE."

— STEPHEN KING

Mobs of obsessed readers flock to Bangor each October, hoping that Stephen King has opened his supposedly haunted Victorian house to the public for Halloween. However, King, who once told Conan O'Brien that he has become the "Santa Claus of Halloween," ended this tradition years ago after it became too overwhelming. Even when it isn't Halloween, fans often loiter on the street outside his home, peering through the wrought iron gate in hopes of catching a glimpse of the famous author.

King's name is synonymous with horror, and his creations have become icons of evil. Bad prom dates evoke references to *Carrie*. Scary dogs are called Cujo. Unusual mishaps involving cars invariably bring mention of *Christine*. "I have been subsumed by the popular culture," King once said, and he isn't entirely happy about it.[1] "I don't want to be on a lunch box," he said recently.[2]

While other writers currently sell as many or more copies of new books as King does (J. K. Rowling and Dan Brown come to mind), no one else symbolizes an entire genre the way King does. News items never say that a court case is like "something out of a John Grisham novel," but hardly a week passes without the media describing a creepy occurrence as "something out of a Stephen King story." Horror novels or films are often said to be "in the tradition of Stephen King."

He almost single-handedly created a booming market for horror fiction where there was none before. In part, it was a matter of being in the right place at the right time. Readers who had experienced the terrors of *Rosemary's Baby* and *The Exorcist* were primed for more, and King delivered. By the time his third novel, *The Shining*, hit the best-seller lists, King was already being called "the master of modern horror." Seemingly overnight, he had become a "brand name" author. However, few of the other writers he identified as his peers in other genres at the time[3] are still household names, which attests to the fact that his success wasn't due only to fortuitous timing. The undeniable brilliance of King's storytelling abilities has propelled him to the top of best-seller lists time and time again. Regardless of the state of the horror genre in the intervening years, King has continued to thrive. He is *sui generis*, a category unto himself.

King has undertaken a unique journey, from a struggling schoolteacher to one of the best-selling—and most

right "Do you know me?" Set photo from King's 1985 American Express commercial.

Undated cemetery photo from King's collection.

recognizable—authors of all time. Over the years, he has embraced every innovation that technology has offered, both in publishing and in generating publicity for his work. In the 1990s, he reinvented the serial novel and experimented with electronic publishing long before it was popular. In the twenty-first century, he is using the Internet, via YouTube promo clips and animated comics, for example, to find new audiences for his work.

In addition to being the author of novels, short stories, and essays, he is a screenwriter, film producer, movie director, and actor. He has appeared in TV commercials, been featured on the cover of *Time* magazine, founded charities, won prestigious awards, and, in recent years, has at last received critical approval for his work.

During the thirty-five years since the publication of *Carrie*, hundreds of millions of copies of King's books have been printed in over thirty languages. Most of his dozens of novels have been filmed, and many of his short stories have been expanded for the big and small screens. Hardly a year has gone by since the mid-1970s without one of King's books appearing on a best-seller list or a film adaptation playing at the cineplex. However, it isn't just brilliant marketing that keeps readers rabid for more; such long-term success can only be attributed to the irresistible grip his writing holds on millions of readers.

While people may feel that they know Stephen King through his extensive body of work, it is important to remember that novelists make things up for a living. Even—perhaps especially—when they are writing autobiographically, they can't resist the temptation to improve on the story. "Whatever happens to us feeds into whatever we write," King has said.[4] But when discussing the relationship between reality and fabrication in his novels, he uses the analogy of a racquetball game: "The fact of the matter is that the ball is almost always in the air," even if it frequently hits the wall that forms the basis in reality for the story.[5]

To completely explore King's life and examine all his novels would require a volume many times larger than this one. However, this book captures many of the events that inspired King's most popular works, using selected novels as a lens through which to observe his life. The previously unpublished personal ephemera that accompany this illustrated companion provide a tangible encounter with the life and creations of the "master of horror."

above PUBLICITY PHOTO OF STEPHEN KING BEHIND THE WHEEL OF A BUICK 8. PHOTO BY AMY GUIP, 2002.

1

THE EARLY YEARS

"BOOKS ARE A UNIQUELY PORTABLE MAGIC." — STEPHEN KING

The legend of Stephen King's sudden arrival on the publishing scene with *Carrie* in 1974 is well known:

How, after spending long hours at a low-paying job teaching high school English, the aspiring novelist, father of two young children, toiled nightly on a typewriter at a child's desk in the furnace room of their rented mobile home.

How he started a short story but discarded it when it grew too long because he didn't think he had the time or the character insight to complete it.

How his wife, Tabitha, fished the pages out of the garbage can, read them, and encouraged him to continue writing it.

How a supportive editor at Doubleday acquired the novel, which was then resold in paperback for enough money that King could quit his day job and write full time.

How, with his very first book, he revitalized a long-dormant genre, changed the face of publishing, and became a cultural phenomenon.

As with all legends, there is some truth, some fantasy, and much oversimplification. The often-told tale above pays short shrift to King's long apprenticeship in publishing. By the time *Carrie* appeared, King had been writing for nearly twenty years and had been a published author for a decade. *Carrie* was not, in fact, King's first novel—it was at least his fifth. The supportive editor, Bill Thompson, had already worked with King on two other novels, but ultimately was unable to convince Doubleday to acquire them.

Stephen King was born in Portland, Maine, on September 21, 1947. His parents, believing they were unable to conceive, had adopted another son, David, who was two at the time of King's birth. Two years later, the boys' father, Donald, abandoned the family and was never heard from again.

Ruth King, their mother, worked at menial jobs to support her family. They moved frequently, living in Wisconsin, Indiana, and Connecticut. King missed most of his first year of school because a case of tonsillitis blossomed into infections that required excruciating ear-lancing procedures. The family didn't own a television, so King had to rely on his imagination to entertain himself during that year, which he spent mostly in bed. He became a voracious reader, and, at the age of six, he started to write.

King's earliest forays into the world of creative fiction involved fashioning prose versions of the comics he was

Ruth King with her two sons, David and Stephen, in Portland, Maine, early 1948.

King and his brother Dave, circa 1953, in their front yard in Fort Wayne, Indiana, where their father's family lived.

STEPHEN AND DAVE IN STRATFORD, CONNECTICUT, 1956.

reading, adding his own descriptions to text he copied verbatim. His mother was charmed until she discovered what he was doing. She told him he should be making up his own stories instead, so he wrote about "four magic animals who rode around in an old car, helping out little kids. Their leader was a large white bunny named Mr. Rabbit Trick. He got to drive the car."[6] His mother told him the story was good enough to be in a book—his first critical review—and she rewarded him with a quarter, his first income from writing.

Ruth King eventually settled in Durham, Maine, which is where King embarked on a series of projects that presaged his future as a creative and innovative force in writing. He

and his new friend Chris Chesley "published" a collection of one-page stories entitled *People, Places & Things* in 1960. Only one of these tales, "The Hotel at the End of the Road," has ever been reprinted, and only a single copy of the original collection exists, owned by King himself.

Around the same time, King also wrote serialized stories for his brother's newspaper, *Dave's Rag*, two of which ("Jumper" and "Rush Call") were reprinted in the Book-of-the-Month Club collection *Secret Windows* in 2000.

In 1961, using his brother Dave's printing press in the basement, King produced a "novelization" of a Roger Corman movie he and Chris had just seen. He figured that if he could

"THEIR LEADER WAS A LARGE WHITE BUNNY NAMED MR. RABBIT TRICK. HE GOT TO DRIVE THE CAR."

left DAVE AND STEPHEN KING, MID-1950s.

ENCLOSED

NEWSPAPER King was the editor of the Lisbon High School newspaper, *The Drum*, during the mid-1960s. He published two short stories and showed his willingness to stretch his talents by contributing illustrations as well. The January 29, 1966, issue of the newspaper contains the only appearance of King's short story "The 43rd Dream" along with a three-panel cartoon.

LETTER A signed letter from fourteen-year-old Stephen King accompanying a short story submission to Forrest Ackerman. His signature is missing the characteristic looping swirl, but is otherwise surprisingly similar to his modern autograph. His submission letter is very mature for someone who is barely a teenager.

COMIC King's first publication was in the fan magazine *Comics Review* issued by Mike Garrett of Birmingham, Alabama. His story "I Was a Teenage Grave Robber" was serialized over several issues of the fanzine in 1965.

King in a lawn chair, mid-1950s.

sell ten copies to his friends at school, the profit after paying for printing supplies and paper would finance his next trip to the movies. If he sold a dozen copies, he could get popcorn and a soda, too.

He exceeded his modest expectations, moving nearly forty copies in one day—until this early venture in self-publishing came to the attention of the school faculty and he was forced to return the $9 in quarters he had collected from his school-mates. King was pleased to discover, however, that many of his customers asked to keep their contraband copies of the book.

By the time he was thirteen, he was confident enough to try submitting his writing for publication. A one-page story called "The Killer" went to Forrest "Forry" Ackerman's *Spaceman* magazine. It wasn't published then, but Ackerman, a legendary packrat, kept the manuscript. Decades later, he asked King to

above AN UNDATED PHOTO FROM THE 1960s SHOWING THE YOUNG MAN WITH HIS DOG.

KING, APPROXIMATELY AGE 14.

KING WITH HIS FIRST CAR, A 1956 PLYMOUTH, ON JUNE 11, 1967,
IN A SHOT CAPTURED BY HIS BROTHER DAVE.

sign the page—King recognized the manuscript immediately because he had handwritten in the letter N throughout because his typewriter was defective. (Ackerman ultimately published "The Killer" in *Famous Monsters of Filmland* magazine in 1994.)

"Codename: Mousetrap" and "The 43rd Dream" were published in 1965 and 1966, respectively, in the Lisbon High School newspaper, *The Drum*, which King edited, though he said of the publication: "*The Drum* did not prosper under my editorship. Then as now, I tend to go through periods of idleness followed by periods of workaholic frenzy."[7] Copies of these issues of the newspaper turned up recently, but the stories have never appeared anywhere else.

King once again fell afoul of the school authorities when he turned his talents to a parody newspaper called *The Village Vomit* that featured fictional tidbits about the school faculty. This time he received two weeks in detention—after he apologized to the offended faculty members. He was also urged to take

a job at the local newspaper. Recognizing his talent and his zeal for writing, his teachers tried to find a way to channel his creative energies.

King began his first novel while a senior in high school, a book called *Getting It On* that would ultimately see publication as *Rage* in 1977 under the pseudonym Richard Bachman. After amassing countless rejection letters from magazines such as *Alfred Hitchcock's Mystery Magazine*, and advancing from form rejections to encouraging personal responses from the likes of science-fiction editor Algis Budrys, "I Was a Teenage Grave Robber"—retitled "In a Half-World of Terror" by the editor—was published in the fanzine *Comics Review* in 1965. Two years later, at the age of twenty, King made his first professional sale, "The Glass Floor," to *Startling Mystery Stories* for $30.

With his poor eyesight, it was unlikely King would have passed the military physical that would have granted him an all-expenses-paid trip to Vietnam, but Ruth King wasn't

above THE YOUNG AUTHOR AT HIS TYPEWRITER, LATE 1960s.

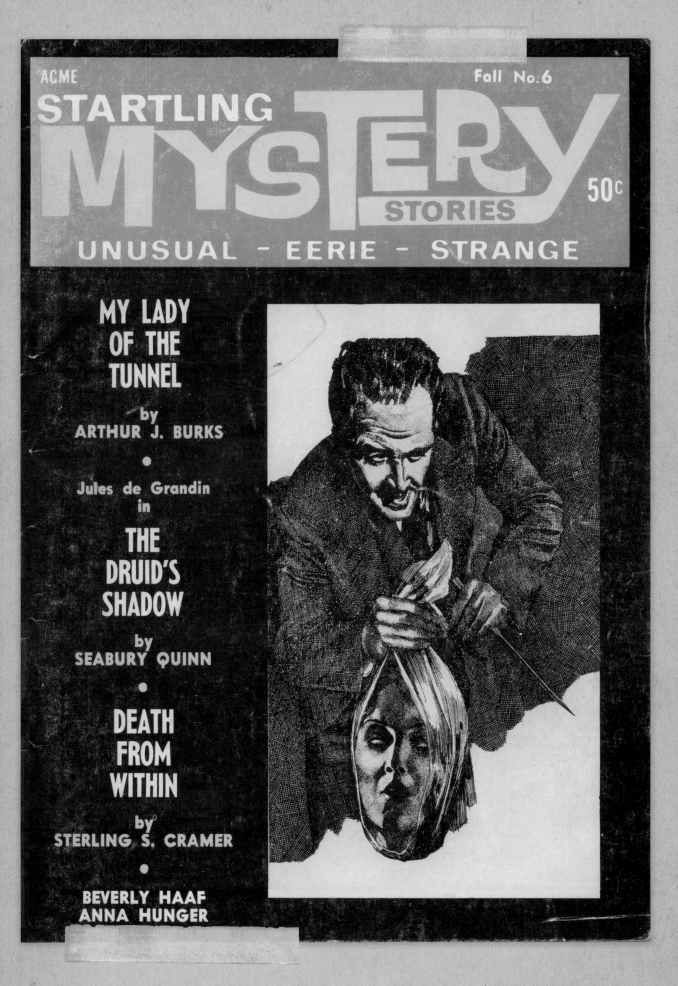

ACME   Fall No. 6

STARTLING
MYSTERY
STORIES

50c

UNUSUAL - EERIE - STRANGE

MY LADY
OF THE
TUNNEL

by
ARTHUR J. BURKS

•

Jules de Grandin
in

THE
DRUID'S
SHADOW

by
SEABURY QUINN

•

DEATH
FROM
WITHIN

by
STERLING S. CRAMER

•

BEVERLY HAAF
ANNA HUNGER

COVER OF THE FALL 1967 ISSUE OF STARTLING MYSTERY STORIES, VOLUME 1, NUMBER 6,
WHICH CONTAINED KING'S FIRST PROFESSIONAL SHORT STORY, "THE GLASS FLOOR."

marsh roots

In fall of 1973, the University of Maine's student literary magazine, Marshroots, printed King's short story "It Grows On You."

fall 1973

volume
three
no. 1

CONTRABAND

...ssue 2 of the literary magazine Contraband (December 1971) contained King's poem "The Hardcase Speaks."

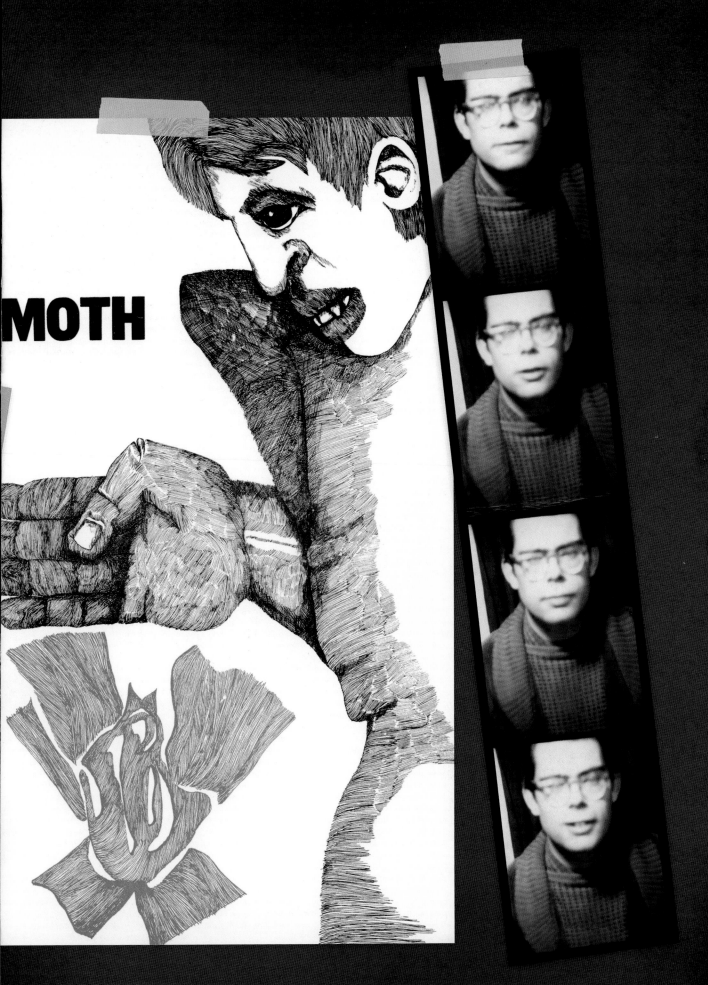

MOTH

MOTH (1970), AN OFF-CAMPUS PUBLICATION THAT CONTAINED KING'S FIRST BOOK APPEARANCE, WHILE HE WAS STILL A STUDENT AT THE UNIVERSITY. IT INCLUDES THREE POEMS BY "STEVE": "THE DARK MAN," "DONOVAN'S BRAIN," AND "SILENCE."

PHOTO-BOOTH PICTURES OF KING TAKEN IN THE LATE 1960s.

taking any chances. She insisted that her son go to college. He attended the University of Maine with scholarships and loans, and continued to write while working odd jobs on and off campus. While a freshman, he entered *The Long Walk* in a first-novel competition, but the submission was rejected without comment.

He started selling his stories to men's magazines such as *Cavalier*, bringing in as much as $200 each—an impressive amount even by today's standards. He snipped the stories out of the magazines and blacked out any sexually explicit ads before sending copies to his mother. He also wrote poetry and short stories for the University of Maine's literary magazines (copies of these rare publications now routinely sell to King collectors for hundreds of dollars). For the *Maine Campus* newspaper,

King serialized a western parody called "Slade," a humorous precursor to his Dark Tower series, and wrote a regular column called "King's Garbage Truck," an antecedent to his current "Pop of King" essays in *Entertainment Weekly*.

The University of Maine was also where Stephen King met Tabitha Spruce, during a picnic for library employees. It was her laugh, which he describes as raucous, wonderful, and unafraid, that first caught his attention—along with the prettiest legs he had ever seen. He says that he fell in love with her partly because he understood what she was doing with the poetry she presented during a workshop class they shared, and partly because *she* understood what she was doing with her work.

King has such a reputation as a horror writer that people sometimes refuse to believe that certain movies adapted from his works have anything to do with him. The producers of *Stand By Me*, based on his novella *The Body Different Seasons*, did not use King's name to promote the film because they didn't want audiences to think it was a horror movie. The change of title further underscores the reasoning behind their decision. Two other well-known movies, *The Green Mile* and *The Shawshank Redemption*, are also not widely recognized as adaptations of King's work. However, it's one thing for people to debate this among themselves and another for someone to argue the point with the author himself, which happened to King when he was in a grocery store in Florida picking up a few necessities. He later recounted the scenario to an interviewer:

This woman comes up to me and she goes, "I know who you are." I guess she's about eighty; she's got that orange hair. She says, "I know who you are! You're that horror writer. You're Stephen King." I said, "Yes, guilty as charged." She said, "I don't read what you do. I respect what you do, but I don't read it. Why don't you do something uplifting sometime, like that Shawshank Redemption*?" I said, "I did write that." She said, "No, you didn't." It was surreal. It was like, "What question have you never been asked? What clothes have you never worn? What person did you never meet?" It was weird.[8]*

They were married a year and a half later, in 1971. King wore a borrowed suit that was too large for him to the ceremony. By the third year of their marriage, they had two children; both parents were forced to work at low-paying jobs to support the family. Unable to find a teaching position, King worked at an industrial laundry (one of the same jobs his mother had held and also the inspiration for his story "The Mangler"), and Tabitha worked at a Dunkin' Donuts.

Their combined income was barely enough to support them, and frequent crises, such as an ailment afflicting one of the children, stretched their budget past its breaking point. At those critical times, King recalls that checks would arrive to save the day—payments for the short stories he was now regularly selling to the men's magazines.

King ultimately landed a teaching job at the Hampden Academy in Maine. The starting salary of $6,400 a year seemed like a huge jump from his minimum wage hourly pay at the laundry, but the amount of extracurricular work involved at the school ate into his writing time. "By most Friday afternoons I felt as if I'd spent the week with jumper cables clamped to my brain," he recalls.[9]

The family, still struggling financially, lived in a rented mobile home at the time. King was, by now, submitting novels to Bill Thompson at Doubleday. He sent the *Getting It On* manuscript to "the editor of *The Parallax View*." It was passed along to Thompson, who remembers the book as "a masterful study in character and suspense, but it was quiet, deliberately claustrophobic and it proved a tough sell within the house."[10] He requested three rewrites, but was ultimately forced to pass on it. *The Long Walk* met with a similar fate, and *The Running Man* didn't generate any interest from the editor. Discouraged, King didn't even bother sending Thompson a book called *Blaze*.

Unable to come up with a new idea, King revisited a short story he had started the previous year. The tale of a bullied teenage girl with telekinetic powers was a response to a friend's challenge to write from a female perspective.

This is for Tabby, who got me into it--and then bailed me out of it.

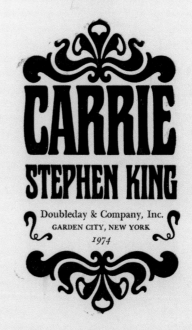

CARRIE
STEPHEN KING

Doubleday & Company, Inc.
GARDEN CITY, NEW YORK
1974

This is for Tabby, who forced me into it.

3rd Draft

SECOND- AND THIRD-
DRAFT DEDICATION PAGES
FOR CARRIE (TITLE PAGE, TOP
RIGHT). THE VERSION
FROM THE SECOND DRAFT
IS THE ONE THAT ULTIMATELY
APPEARED IN THE NOVEL.

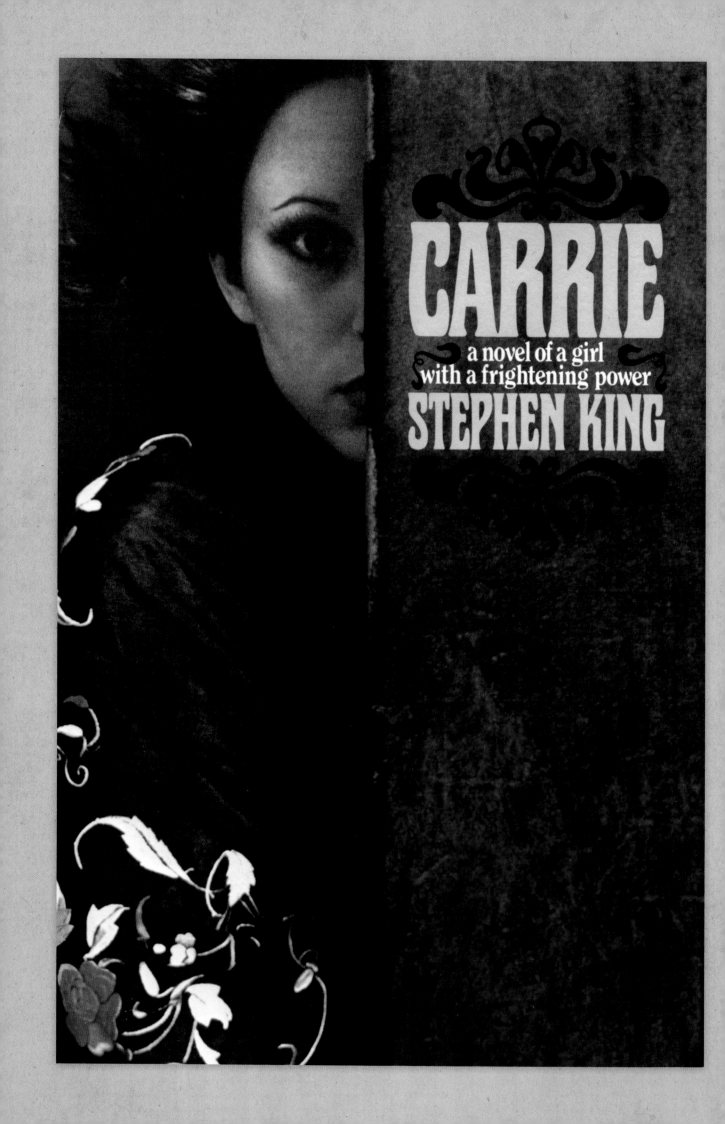

"I SUDDENLY FELT THAT I HAD TO BUY TABBY A MOTHER'S DAY PRESENT, SOMETHING WILD AND EXTRAVAGANT. I TRIED, BUT HERE'S ONE OF LIFE'S TRUE FACTS: THERE'S NOTHING REALLY WILD AND EXTRAVAGANT FOR SALE AT LAVERDIERE'S."

Hoping for something that would yield a quick paycheck from a magazine, King stopped working on it when he realized the story needed a "longer fuse before the explosion."[11] He didn't think he had the luxury of time it would take to write another novel. King also felt that he didn't know enough about teenage girls to finish the book: "I was making my entry into a woman's world where I would have to deal with many things I'd never considered before."[12]

The part of the legend where Tabitha rescued four single-spaced pages from the trash is true, yet she also helped in other ways. "Several times during the course of that book Tabby was able to supply doorways at crucial moments," King recalled in an interview.[13]

He finished the manuscript, but had so little faith in it, and was so dejected by his near misses with Doubleday, that he decided not to send it to Thompson. There didn't seem to be much of a market for horror novels at the time.

However, Thompson later sent King a country music calendar to reestablish contact, which encouraged King to submit *Carrie*. Dave King once heard his brother say that if *Carrie* had come six months earlier or six months later, he might have missed out on the perfect timing presented by the popularity of *The Exorcist*, and he would still be teaching English.[14]

After a round of revisions, concentrating primarily on the book's last fifty pages, Doubleday purchased the novel. Word of the sale came by telegram, since the Kings had removed their phone to save money. King says that what he remembers best about the telegram were the final four words: "Bingo. *Carrie* officially a Doubleday book. $2500 against royalties. Call for glorious details. The future lies ahead."[15]

The advance of $2,500 was a fairly low figure even in 1973. It was just enough to buy a Ford Pinto to replace their car, which had just lost its transmission. (The Pinto featured prominently in one of his later works: *Cujo*.) To celebrate the sale, King borrowed $75 from his wife's grandmother for an all-night bus ride from Maine to New York City to meet his editor for the first time.

Disappointingly, the advance wasn't sufficient for King to give up his teaching job. However, he told Tabitha that the paperback rights might sell for as much as $60,000—enough to keep the family running for three or four years if they were frugal, during which time he could write another four or five novels. They decided it was worth a shot.

Then, on Mother's Day 1973 came the fateful call (by now the Kings had a telephone again). Doubleday had sold the paperback rights to Signet for $400,000, the equivalent of nearly $2 million in today's dollars, half of which would go to King.

He was alone in their apartment when he got the news. He remembers, "The only store that was open on Bangor's Main Street was LaVerdiere's Drug. I suddenly felt that I had to buy Tabby a Mother's Day present, something wild and extravagant. I tried, but here's one of life's true facts: there's nothing really wild and extravagant for sale at LaVerdiere's. I did the best I could. I got her a hair-dryer."[16] He also recalls experiencing a rush of paranoia, sure that he would be killed by a car while crossing the street on the way home.

In a bittersweet twist, King's mother lived long enough to hear the news of her son's success, but died of cancer before *Carrie* was released in 1974. However, she must have gained some satisfaction from knowing that, after writing over 1,500 pages of manuscripts, her son was finally a published novelist.

---

left DOUBLEDAY HARDCOVER EDITION OF CARRIE.

Editor Bill Thompson is credited with discovering two famous authors. The first was Stephen King, when Thompson was with Doubleday in the 1970s. Thompson's encouragement kept King writing, even after three novels, two of which underwent extensive rewrites, failed to generate a contract. But Thompson knew that the fourth book was the charm: "I don't think at any time before or after have I as editor been so in tune with the author's concept of a book. Steve and I knew what *Carrie* was supposed to do for and to the reader."[17]

Thompson bumped the approved advance of $1,500 up to $2,500 and sneaked it past the accountants and contract writers. He edited King's next four books. However, when King decided to sever his relationship with Doubleday at the end of the 1970s, Thompson was released by the publisher.

However, he remained close to King during the ensuing years. While at his new position with Everest House, Thompson suggested that King write a nonfiction book about the horror phenomenon. Though it sounded like a lot of work, he convinced King it would make his life easier. Whenever anyone asked him why he wrote horror—or why people read it—all he would have to do is direct them to *Danse Macabre*. "You'll sell books and never have to answer those questions again!" Thompson told him.[18]

In 1987, a manuscript from a Mississippi lawyer landed on Thompson's desk at Wynwood Press, where he was working at the time. The book, which had already been rejected by numerous publishers, was called *A Time to Kill* and its author was John Grisham. Thompson arranged for an advance of $15,000 and a first printing of 5,000 copies. Grisham's debut didn't fare as well as *Carrie* did—there were no huge paperback deals or movie options—but it was his break into publication. His second novel, which Thompson also edited, was *The Firm*, the book that launched Grisham's career to bestselling status.

DEPT 109 DOUBDAY

BKN   PD

STEPHEN KING
RFD # 2 , BOX 499D
CARMEL, MAINE 04419

BINGO. CARRIE OFFICIALLY A DOUBLEDAY BOOK. $2500 AGAINST
ROYALTIES. CALL FOR GLORIOUS DETAILS. CONGRATULATIONS. LOVE
THE FUTURE LIES AHEAD.

BILL THOMPSON
DOUBDAY
277 PARK AVE
NEW YORK

BILL THOMPSON'S TELEGRAM TO KING ANNOUNCING CARRIE'S SALE.

April 20, 1973

Mr. William G. Thompson
Doubleday and Company, Inc.
277 Park Avenue
New York, N.Y. 10017

Dear Bill,

I've gotten the contracts with the filled-in payment clause, and
have initialed them both--good show. Now if Carrie will only bring
in a million dollars and set me up for life...I can see myself in
a big yella Cadillac with pink fuzz on the steering wheel and a pair
of baby shoes dangling from the rear-view mirror; built-in four-
channel stereo tape deck, antelope antlers on the hood, and all that
jazz. Gawd, ain't capitalism wonderful? Who says I'm a disassociated
young writer?

Seriously, I can't wait to get the re-typed copy of Carrie and nail
down the script changes we talked about. I've played with a couple
of possible additions, and have decided against them. There is a
temptation to go on fooling with things right into infinity.

We've got a whole houseful of candles lit--I hope you can sell the
rights forty different ways, including bubble-gum cards (on second
thought, forget the cards).

Say hello to everyone at your end.

Best,

Stephen King

PS-My God, how can anyone support the Mets with the Yankees in town?

LETTER FROM KING TO BILL THOMPSON REGARDING HIS PUBLISHING
CONTRACT FOR THE HARDCOVER EDITION OF CARRIE.

2 ROOM 217

"THIS INHUMAN PLACE MAKES HUMAN MONSTERS."

THE SHINING

King's proceeds from the paperback version and film rights for *Carrie* finally afforded him the ability to quit his day job and write full time. When Brian De Palma's movie adaptation appeared, it inspired over a million people to buy the paperback. However, if King turned out to be a one-hit wonder, that money—though it was far more than he had ever seen in his life—wouldn't last forever.

As a follow-up to *Carrie*, King gave Bill Thompson two manuscripts to consider—*Roadwork*, later published as a Bachman novel, and *Second Coming* (subsequently retitled *'Salem's Lot)*, the story of vampires infiltrating a small Maine town. Though vampires have become overused in contemporary horror fiction, King is credited with divesting them of their traditional Gothic settings. In one fell swoop, he both modernized and Americanized horror. The paperback edition of *'Salem's Lot* earned an advance of $500,000 (again, split with Doubleday). When it became his first best-seller, King's future as a full-time writer at last seemed assured.

The Kings moved to Boulder, Colorado, on a whim in 1974— a finger stab at a map of the United States determined their

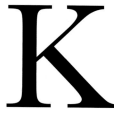

SECOND COMING
By Stephen King

above TITLE PAGE FROM KING'S FIRST DRAFT OF 'SALEM'S LOT.

DRACULA COMES TO 'SALEM'S LOT

Stephen King first read *Dracula* when he was eleven and rediscovered the book almost fifteen years later when he was teaching an elective high school course called Fantasy and Science Fiction. Over dinner one night with Tabitha and his long-time friend Chris Chesley, the topic turned to how differently things might have transpired if Dracula had come to America in the 1970s instead of turn-of-the-century London.

Details of the dinner conversation have changed over the years. In one version, King joked that Dracula would "land in New York and be killed by a taxicab, like Margaret Mitchell in Atlanta."[19] In another, he postulated, "such a vampire would survive perhaps three weeks before Efram Zimbalist, Jr. and the FBI showed up and dragged him off, a victim of wiretaps and God knows what other modern surveillance."[20]

Regardless of what King actually said, it was the response of his dinner companions that resonated with him. What if, instead of a major metropolis, Dracula came to rural Maine, a place that is so isolated that almost anything could happen there? He thought, "People could drop out of sight, disappear, perhaps even come back as the living dead."[21]

Among King's other influences for *'Salem's Lot* were *Peyton Place* by Grace Metalious and Thornton Wilder's *Our Town*, the latter of which King also happened to be teaching at the time. He felt a contemporary setting for his own story would work in the vampire's favor, because "electric lights and modern inventions would actually aid the incubus, by rendering belief in him all but impossible."[22]

POSSIBLY THE REAL-LIFE INSPIRATION FOR THE HAUNTED HOUSE IN 'SALEM'S LOT, THIS PHOTO FROM KING'S ALBUM IS LABELED "MARSTEN HOUSE."

KING'S CAMEO IN THE SHINING MINISERIES WAS AS GAGE CREED, THE GHOSTLY CONDUCTOR OF THE EQUALLY PHANTASMAL ORCHESTRA IN THE OVERLOOK HOTEL'S BALLROOM.

destination, according to one version of the story. They drove west to a rented house where King hoped to write his next novel, a *roman à clef* called *The House on Value Street*, loosely based on Patty Hearst's kidnapping by the Symbionese Liberation Army.

That fall, King and his wife left their two children with a babysitter for a brief getaway at the Stanley Hotel in Estes Park, forty miles north of Boulder. They arrived on the night before the hotel closed for the winter and were its only guests. The dining room was still open, but only one entrée was being served. The chairs were turned upside down atop every table except theirs. The tuxedo-clad orchestra played for them and them alone.

The empty hotel struck King as the archetypal setting for a ghost story. He encountered many of *The Shining*'s iconic images as he wandered the corridors after his wife went to bed, including a bartender named Grady and a clawfoot bathtub that looked like someone could die in it—or already had. Later, he dreamed of his young son, Joe, screaming as a fire hose chased him down the hotel's endless hallways. By the end of the night, King had the story outline mapped out in his head.

The book developed from a combination of several ideas; the visit to the Stanley simply helped bring them all together. For years, King had been toying with an idea about a boy with the power to make dreams become real, inspired by the nursery

THE STANLEY HOTEL

F. O. Stanley, inventor of the Stanley Steamer automobile, built the Stanley Hotel between 1907 and 1909. Unlike *The Shining*'s Overlook Hotel, the Stanley is not isolated. It is perched on a hillside above the town of Estes Park, Colorado.

When it came time to readapt the novel as a television miniseries, King and director Mick Garris decided to film on location. King had previously stated in interviews that the Stanley had been turned into time-sharing condominiums, which proved untrue. The production team restored parts of the hotel to their original glory as part of the deal that allowed them to use the site. Digital effects removed any nearby buildings that made it into camera range.

King's novel and the adaptations have raised the hotel's profile as a haunted destination. Teams of ghost hunters have filmed their paranormal investigations, declaring the hotel the second-most haunted in the United States. Most of the activity is said to take place on the fourth floor, two stories above the famous room 217.

The proprietors hasten to explain that any supernatural presences belong to "good spirits." One of the ghosts is supposed to be Lord Dunraven, who sold the land for the hotel to Stanley. However, he left Colorado in the 1880s, so how his ghost ended up back there is anyone's guess.

The hotel shown in Stanley Kubrick's adaptation was a combination of exteriors shot at the Timberline Lodge in Mount Hood, Oregon, and interiors constructed on a sound stage in England. Although Kubrick's film was not shot at the Stanley Hotel, the owners permanently loop it on a closed-circuit TV channel. Netflix even set up an outdoor projection system on the Colorado hotel's grounds in 2006 and hosted an "on-site" viewing for over a thousand people from across the United States.

THE STANLEY HOTEL IN ESTES PARK, COLORADO, KING'S INSPIRATION FOR THE OVERLOOK HOTEL.

FATHER WHO?

Collectors rarely have to worry about more than the condition of a book's dust jacket and the price listed on the flap when assessing the value of a first edition. The price is a reliable indicator of when the dust jacket was printed. Unscrupulous sellers have been known to mate later dust jackets with first printing books to raise their value.

The situation with King's second novel, *'Salem's Lot*, is a little more complex, however. Shortly before the book was published, Doubleday decided to reduce its price from $8.95 to $7.95. Rather than face the expense of reprinting the dust jackets, the corner containing the price was clipped.

However, what the publisher didn't notice was that the dust jacket copy on the inner flap referenced a character named Father Cody instead of Father Callahan. Jimmy Cody was a doctor in the book. At some point, the error was caught and corrected.

The value of a first edition of *'Salem's Lot* depends on which of the three dust jackets it wears. Only five copies of the variant with the original $8.95 price are known to exist.

Among King's other influences for *The Shining* were Edgar Allen Poe's "The Fall of the House of Usher" and "The Masque of the Red Death"—a passage from the latter is used as one of the book's epigraphs. Shirley Jackson's novels *The Haunting of Hill House* and *The Sundial* also worked their way into *The Shining*; hotel chef Dick Halloran's name is an allusion to the Halloran house from *The Sundial*.

Since their rental house in Boulder was rather small, King leased office space in a boardinghouse where he could look out the window at the Flatiron Mountains. He remembers that, once he started working on the book, he entered a zone where everything he wrote worked: "The story unspooled itself without a hitch or a snag. I never had that depressing feeling that I had lost my way."[24] He averaged 3,000 words per day, and the first draft required the least rewriting of all of his early books. King felt himself "mesmerized by the story, my conscious mind little more than a conduit for feelings that flowed, almost whole, from my subconscious."[25]

Though the writing came fast, the process of putting into words the story of a man isolated with his family drew King back to his days of poverty. "For much of the three or four months it took me to write the first draft," King recalls, "I seemed to be back in that trailer in Hermon, Maine, with no company but the buzzing sound of the snowmobiles and my own fears—fears that my chance to be a writer had come and gone, fears that I had gotten into a teaching job that was completely wrong for me, fears most of all that my marriage was edging onto marshy ground and that there might be quicksand anyplace ahead."[26]

King was already a heavy drinker by this point in his life. Struggling to support his family while trying to break through as a writer had taken its toll, as did his mother's death. In interviews, he confessed to feeling rage toward his family—and guilt over the anger—but he often didn't make a direct connection between himself and Jack Torrance until after he became sober. "I found myself sometimes pregnant with sordid, unromantic emotions I had never

in Ray Bradbury's short story "The Veldt." That novel, which was to be called *Darkshine*, was set in an amusement park. However, King couldn't come up with a legitimate reason why the characters wouldn't simply flee from the park screaming for help "once the bogeys began oozing from the woodwork."[23] A snowbound hotel solved that problem.

right DOUBLEDAY HARDCOVER EDITION OF THE SHINING.

The Shining

by
Stephen King

A new novel
by the
author of
CARRIE
and
'SALEM'S LOT

"BY MAKING JACK TORRANCE A DRINKER . . . I FOUND MYSELF ABLE TO LOOK AROUND A DARK CORNER AND TO SEE MYSELF AS I COULD HAVE BEEN, UNDER THE RIGHT SET OF CIRCUMSTANCES."

suspected, some directed toward my wife, some toward my children—they ranged from impatience to anger to outright hate," King later admitted. "By making Jack Torrance a drinker . . . I found myself able to look around a dark corner and to see myself as I could have been, under the right set of circumstances."[27]

Fifteen years after that visit to the Stanley Hotel, King wrote about his revelation one night when counting the empty beer bottles that had accumulated in the recycling bin in only a few days: "I'm an alcoholic, I thought, and there was no dissenting opinion from inside my head—I was, after all, the guy who had

written *The Shining* without even realizing (at least until that night) that I was writing about myself."[28]

Like the Kings, the Torrance family flees to Colorado from New England. However, the reason for their exodus is less lofty. Instead of having the luxury of seeking a new setting to inspire his writing, Jack Torrance is desperate. The son of an abusive father, he's battling alcohol and anger, has already broken his son's arm in a blind rage, lost his job at a posh prep school after hitting one of his students, and may have killed someone in a drunk-driving incident. He's unemployed, his writing isn't going anywhere, his five-year-old son, Danny,

left A Doubleday promotional photo of King, circa 1975, by Alex Gotfryd. above The Torrence family escapes to Colorado in Stanley Kubrick's film adaptation of The Shining. Shelley Duvall as Wendy, Danny Lloyd as Danny, and Jack Nicholson as Jack Torrence.

is exhibiting emotional problems, and if his mother-in-law weren't the greater of two evils, his wife, Wendy, would have left him already. Taking a job as the winter caretaker of the Overlook Hotel is one of the few last straws left for Jack to grasp.

Jack sees his potential as a "blooming American writer" with a story published in *Esquire* slipping away. Teaching left him little time to devote to his own work, but once that job was gone he started concentrating on drinking instead of writing. He intends to spend his snowbound months in the empty hotel finishing a play called "The Little School." Wendy is happy that he is writing again, thinking that he "seemed to be slowly closing a huge door on a roomful of monsters." She has no idea what is in store for them in the Overlook.

In the grand Gothic tradition, the Overlook is a bad place—a "haunted hotel, with a different 'real' horror movie playing in almost every one of its guest room and suites."[29] King saw it as "a huge storage battery charged with an evil powerful enough to corrupt all those who come into contact with it."[30] The evil derives from a century of horrific incidents that have taken place within its walls. "With my rigorous Methodist upbringing, I began to wonder if the haunted house could not be turned into a kind of symbol of unexpiated sin," King wrote.[31] In *The Shining*'s introduction, he asks the reader, "Aren't memories

Tony Zavarelli
Director
Wholesale Sales

SEPTEMBER, 1977

DEAR NAL WHOLESALER:

"THE SHINING"
. OVER 200,000 HARDCOVER SALES
. LITERARY GUILD FULL SELECTION
. NEW YORK TIMES BESTSELLER
. BESTSELLER ON NATIONAL AND LOCAL LISTS
. EXCELLENT REVIEWS IN COSMOPOLITAN, CHICAGO TRIBUNE
  BOOK WORLD, LOS ANGELES MAGAZINE, CHICAGO TRIBUNE,
  NEW YORK TIMES
. MAJOR STANLEY KUBRICK MOVIE STARRING JACK NICHOLSON IN LATE 1978

STEPHEN KING
. MASTER OF THE MODERN HORROR STORY
. AUTHOR OF "CARRIE"
    . Pre-movie tie-in, 1,476,000 copies sold
    . Movie tie-in, 1,524,000 copies sold
    . Total of 2,900,000 copies sold
. AUTHOR OF "'SALEM'S LOT"
    . 2,200,000 copies sold
.OVER 5,100,000 SIGNET STEPHEN KING BOOKS SOLD

N A L
. BIGGEST RADIO AD CAMPAIGN IN NAL'S HISTORY REACHING 58 MILLION CONSUMERS
. A HUGE $100,000 WILL BE SPENT FOR THIS EXTENSIVE PROMOTION OF "THE SHINING"
. EXCITING RADIO AD WILL BE MADE AVAILABLE TO WHOLESALERS HAVING ADVERTISING
  TRADE-OFF ARRANGEMENTS WITH LOCAL RADIO PEOPLE
. SUBWAY ADS IN MAJOR MARKETS
. EXTENSIVE TRADE ANNOUNCEMENTS IN CPDA NEWS, PUBLISHERS WEEKLY AND PROFIT WAYS
. LOTS OF POINT-OF-SALE STUFF
    . Exciting floor displays with dynamite special riser cards
    . Easy-to-place counter displays
    . Striking silver lip cards
    . "THE SHINING" T-shirts for retailers in-store promotions
    . National WATS line for retailers to call and hear our dramatic radio ad
    . Super contest for your promotion and routemen

"THE SHINING" . . . SIGNET'S HUGE JANUARY BLOCKBUSTER . . . WATCH FOR IT!!!

                    TERRIFYINGLY YOURS,

                    Tony

                    TONY ZAVARELLI

TZ/lm

THE SHINING
A MASTERPIECE OF MODERN HORROR BY
STEPHEN KING

New American Library, P.O. Box 120, Bergenfield, New Jersey 07621

LETTER SENT TO BOOKSELLERS BY NAL ANNOUNCING THE PUBLICITY
CAMPAIGN FOR THE PAPERBACK EDITION OF THE SHINING.

ENCLOSED

TITLE PAGE Dated May 13, 1975, this draft of the title page still bears King's original title, *The Shine*, along with a handwritten note to Bill Thompson admonishing the editor not to lose it, as it was the only copy.

MANUSCRIPT PAGES Three pages from the original manuscript show how King changed his mind about Danny's encounter with the fire hose outside room 217 in Chapter 19. In the first draft, King leaves no doubt in the reader's mind that the hose chased Danny, while in the published version, it's all in Danny's mind. The first draft of "Inside 217"—the famous bathtub scene—contains King's handwritten revisions and annotations. In this draft, Danny's mother is named Jenny.

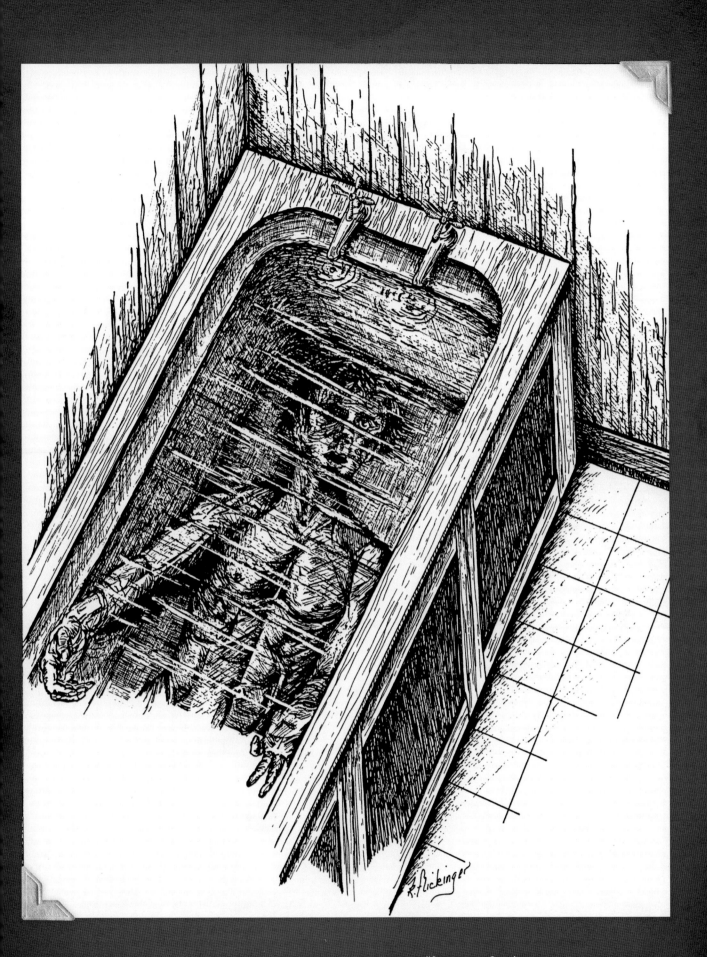

"TONER IN THE TUB" BY KATHERINE FLICKINGER DEPICTS A SCENE FROM "BEFORE THE PLAY," THE PROLOGUE TO
THE SHINING THAT WAS CUT PRIOR TO PUBLICATION, IN WHICH LEWIS TONER, THE SPURNED LOVER OF THE
OVERLOOK'S OWNER, HORACE DERWENT, COMMITS SUICIDE IN HIS HOTEL ROOM BATHTUB IN THE 1930s.

⊕ The Overlook was At Home with the Dead ⊕

"The Overlook Hotel was At Home with the Dead" by Katherine Flickinger, created for The Shape Under the Sheet: The Complete Stephen King Encyclopedia by Stephen Spignesi.

The Overlook Hotel

the true ghosts of our lives? Do they not drive us all to words and acts we regret from time to time?"[32]

Jack Torrance's weakness of character makes him vulnerable to the hotel's evil. It is an open question whether he would have survived the winter trapped with his family even without the evil influence of the Overlook. Long before the family arrives there, he's the poster child for a violent meltdown—the kind of man who appears in newspaper headlines for committing suicide after cracking under financial or emotional pressure and killing his own family. All he needs is one more bad thing to happen to push him over the edge.

Jack Torrance is miserable, depressed, and self-destructive, but he's trying his best to succeed. Left to his own devices, he might have survived. The Overlook doesn't give him a chance, though—his inner evils are trumped by the supernatural power of the hotel. In the book's introduction, King says, "I believe these [horror] stories exist because we sometimes need to create unreal monsters and bogies to stand in for all the things we fear in our real lives."[33]

His hope, though, is that "you don't get scared of monsters— you get scared for people."[34] This succinctly describes one of the secrets of King's success—his books are fundamentally about how people react to stressful circumstances. He makes readers care for his characters, and then throws something catastrophic at them.

Jack's decision to abandon his play to write the Overlook's history after he becomes obsessed with documents he finds in the cellar is an apt metaphor for the way he can't escape his own past. King considers Jack a fundamentally good person who succumbs to the terrible attraction of violence.[35]

above THE OVERLOOK HOTEL" BY KATHERINE FLICKINGER, CREATED FOR THE SHAPE UNDER THE SHEET: THE COMPLETE STEPHEN KING ENCYCLOPEDIA BY STEPHEN SPIGNESI.

That quality makes him a "more realistic (and perhaps more frightening) character," [36] because he isn't simply a man who was motivated to commit crimes by supernatural forces. Jack is part of a vicious cycle of abuse, weakened by his love for a father who beat his mother, and perversely determined to pass this curse on to his son. "Jack Torrance himself is a haunted house," King says. "He's haunted by his father."[37]

It's not surprising that King has an ambivalent attitude toward fathers, given the fact that his own abandoned the family when he was two. He later reflected in an interview, "I was encountering fatherhood from my end and I'd never experienced it from any other end—that is, being a child and having a father and going on fishing trips and all the rest of that stuff."[38]

Though Jack seems to be the hotel's primary target, its real goal is Jack's son, Danny, who has impressive extrasensory powers. His mother is a strong, independent woman (unlike the dishrag played by Shelley Duvall in Stanley Kubrick's film adaptation). When confronted by the reality of her situation—trapped miles from civilization with a man who is undergoing a breakdown in a hotel that also happens to be haunted—she doesn't surrender the way Jack does. Her determination to survive and resist the

evils, natural and supernatural, allows her and Danny to make it out alive against terrible odds.

King structured the book like a five-act Shakespearean play, "a kind of inside-out *King Lear*, where Lear is this young guy who has a son instead of daughters."[39] The first draft had scenes instead of chapters and ended with Wendy and Danny escaping from the hotel on a snowmobile with Dick Halloran. Feeling that there were too many loose ends in this version, King added an epilogue and later, for balance, wrote a lengthy prologue that detailed the hotel's checkered past. As a cost-saving measure, Doubleday removed the prologue and epilogue; the final chapter of the published book contains the only part of the epilogue that survives. The prologue was published in *Whispers* magazine in 1982 and later abridged in *TV Guide* when the miniseries adaptation aired on ABC.

King's original title for the book, *The Shine*, came from John Lennon's song "Instant Karma," but Doubleday changed it because "shine" was deemed a pejorative term for African Americans. King said that he could live with the new title but found it "rather unwieldy and thudding."[40] However, the subsequent success of *The Shining* inspired countless horror novels with titles consisting of "The" followed by a gerund, used by authors and publishers hoping to strike the same winning chord that *The Shining* had.

King's current assessment of the book is mixed: "There is a cocky quality to some of *The Shining*'s prose that has come to grate on me in later years, but I still like the book enormously."[41] His editor, Bill Thompson, wasn't initially thrilled by King's description of the book, either, fearing that it was going to forever brand King as a horror writer. However, after actually reading the manuscript, Thompson was decidedly enthusiastic.

The Shining became King's first hardcover bestseller, reaching number eight on the *New York Times* list and selling roughly 50,000 copies.[42] To this day, it is almost universally acknowledged as a modern classic that will probably be one of the seminal works that King will be remembered for in generations to come.

above AUTHOR PHOTO FOR CARRIE BY ALEX GOTFRYD, WHO ALSO TOOK KING'S PHOTO FOR THE SHINING.

DEAR MR. KING,

FOR THE FIRST TIME SINCE I'VE PICKED UP "THE SHINING", I'VE FINALLY BEEN AT PEACE. MY LAST THREE NIGHTS SLEEP HAVE BEEN DISTURBED BY MONSTERS IN THE NIGHT & THINGS CRAWLING INTO MY BED WHEN THE LIGHTS GO OUT.

FINALLY, JACK TAKES A DRINK. (I AM AT EASE). IS IT, OR ISN'T IT?

YOUR BOOK STARES AT ME FROM MY 60 WATT LAMP. PLEASE TELL ME WHETHER I SHOULD GO ON OR NOT. MY SANITY IS AT STAKE.

Jon

A FAN LETTER TO KING CONCERNING THE SHINING.

3

THE WALKIN' DUDE

"AND THE RIGHTEOUS AND UNRIGHTEOUS ALIKE WERE
CONSUMED IN THAT HOLY FIRE."

THE STAND

In 1969, Stephen King published a short story called "Night Surf" in the University of Maine literary magazine *Ubris*. He reworked it extensively before selling it to *Cavalier* five years later.

"Night Surf" is about a group of teenagers who have survived a virus called A6 that has decimated the population. They believe they are immune, but as the story develops, some of them begin to show symptoms of the disease, which they call "Captain Trips." King wanted to tell a longer story about the world after the virus, but he didn't feel ready to write it at that time.

After he finished *The Shining*, he wrote the novella *Apt Pupil*, then decided to return to his Patty Hearst novel, *The House on Value Street*. He spent six weeks on it, but it wasn't coming together.

Then, King read about an accident in Utah where canisters of a chemical more deadly than Agent Orange fell from a truck, split open, and killed some sheep. The news accounts hinted that, if the wind had been blowing in a different direction, a toxic cloud might have threatened Salt Lake City. The incident reminded him of *Earth Abides*, a novel by George R. Stewart in which a virus destroys most of the world's population. Still

determined to write about Hearst, he wondered what would happen if the members of the Symbionese Liberation Army became immune to the disease for some reason.

A short while later, news bulletins about the first-ever outbreak of Legionnaires' disease emerged from Philadelphia. When he heard a radio preacher utter the phrase, "once in every generation, the plague will fall among them," he liked it enough to write it down and post it on his desk.

A photograph of one of the SLA members further stoked his imagination. In the picture, Donald Defreeze was wearing a large hat that cloaked his features in shadow. To King, he was a "dark man" with no face, a phrase that resonated back to a poem of the same name that King had published in 1970.

King finally gave up on Patty Hearst and started a two-year trek across America with the survivors of the superflu. He approached the destruction of over ninety-nine percent of the population with glee: "Much of the compulsion I felt while writing *The Stand* obviously came from envisioning an entire entrenched societal process destroyed at a stroke."[43] He saw the superflu as an unusual solution to the energy crisis. People wouldn't have to line up at gas stations any more. The Cold War would end, pollution would abate, and the planet would get a

UBRIS

COVER OF THE SPRING 1969 EDITION OF <u>UBRIS</u>, WHICH CONTAINED KING'S SHORT STORY, "NIGHT SURF," WHERE HE FIRST MENTIONS THE VIRUS CAPTAIN TRIPS.

STEPHEN KING

THE
STAND

DOUBLEDAY & COMPANY, INC., GARDEN CITY, NEW YORK
1979

ORIGINAL TITLE LAYOUT PAGE FOR THE STAND, ON VELLUM, FROM THE TYPESCRIPT SETTING COPY.

KING IN THE
LATE 1970s.

breather: "a season of rest," he wrote in his notes.[44] There was a chance for "humanity's remaining shred to start over again in a God-centered world to which miracles, magic, and prophecy had returned."[45]

Writing an epic fantasy with a host of characters—some good, some evil—on a *Lord of the Rings* scale but with an American setting rather than a make-believe land appealed to King. Readers wouldn't need to learn a new language or require maps of a fictitious landscape. The setting would be eerily familiar already.

At first, King started the book from Frannie Goldsmith's perspective as she gathers followers on a trek across the ravaged landscape of the former America, like Dorothy in *The Wizard of Oz*. This approach proved cumbersome, however, so King instead opted to write the novel from multiple viewpoints. The ordeals of the survivors are told in separate chapters until they finally all get together in the west.

Though the first section of the novel is devoted to the way the Captain Trips virus spreads across the country, killing almost everyone in its wake, King was most interested in what

"TO ME, THE ULTIMATE THING ABOUT EVIL IS THAT IT
LEADS NOWHERE. . . . YOU CAN LAUGH EVIL OUT OF EXISTENCE."

would happen in the aftermath. In his mind, the Apollonian faction would concern itself with setting up a social structure and reestablishing fundamental rights, while the Dionysian group on the other side of the mountains would amass weapons for a conflict that both sides realized was inevitable.

He explained once in an interview, "If almost everybody died, think of everything that would be left around . . . nuclear weapons and things like that. You could have a society in Schenectady and another one in a place like Boston, and they could get into a theological argument and end up literally exchanging nuclear weapons. I mean, those things are not that hard to run . . . Might take them a little while, but it wouldn't take them very long."[46]

The Stand is about more than survival, though. The survivors are presented with a moral dilemma: Are they fundamentally good or evil? Do they respond to the summons of the benign Mother Abigail or to that of the dark man, Randall Flagg, the Walkin' Dude? Do they join the Boulder Free Zone or go to Las Vegas, a city King thinks of as fundamentally bland, which even today is sometimes referred to as Sin City?

above Goya's painting "Duel With Clubs," which likely inspired the artwork for the cover of The Stand.

THE STAND

a novel by the author of
THE SHINING

STEPHEN KING

THE DOUBLEDAY HARDCOVER EDITION OF THE STAND.

King recalls, "I started to think about that dichotomy between the spiritual and the technological, and that became the great subject of the book."[47] In later years, he referred to *The Stand* as a "long tale of dark Christianity."[48] The cover, a reinterpretation of a Goya painting, "looks like what the spirit of the book is about," King said.[49]

The Stand is much more optimistic about the post-apocalyptic behavior of people than later King books. Survivors band together into small groups, sharing resources and expertise. Groups merge to form even larger ones, until a society begins to develop again. The only characters that are suspicious of others are those tempted by evil, such as Harold Lauder. Conversely, in *Cell*, which King wrote thirty years later, survivors of a global catastrophe are actively hostile toward one another and rarely associate with people they didn't know before the crisis.

The personification of good in *The Stand* is Mother Abigail, an ancient black woman from Hemingford Home, Nebraska. Countering her is Randall Flagg, a shape-shifting demon of unknown origin who materialized during the height of the epidemic. To King, Flagg was "everything that I know of in the last twenty years that's really bad,"[50] an amalgamation of a number of sociopaths, including Charles Manson, Charles Whitman (who in 1966 shot over forty people on the University of Texas campus in Austin), and Charlie Starkweather (a spree killer who murdered eleven people in Nebraska and Wyoming in 1958).

The book provided King with a sprawling canvas on which to map out his thoughts about the nature of good and evil. King says he doesn't see "good" as a completely Christian force: "It's what I think of as white. White. Just tremendously powerful, something that would run you right over if you got in its way."[51] (He also explored this concept in the Dark Tower series, where the force for good is called ka, an abstract power that impels Roland and his followers to succeed.) On the other hand, King's view of evil is that it is powerful but stupid. Though Randall Flagg is disruptive, his plans almost always fail. King

KING'S FAVORITE SCENE IN *THE STAND*

King's favorite scene in *The Stand* is the part where Larry Underwood and Rita Blakemoor are trying to escape from New York City: "Almost everybody in the country is dead. He gets into an argument with her by the Lincoln Tunnel. The tunnel is jammed both ways with cars whose drivers died before they could get out. The only way out is to walk the two miles through the tunnel, around all the cars, and all the bodies inside. And there are no lights. He starts through the tunnel, alone, and gets about halfway. And he is thinking about all the dead people in their cars and he starts to hear footsteps and car doors opening and closing. I think that's a really wonderful scene. I mean can you imagine that poor guy?"[52]

says, "A lot of people were disappointed in *The Stand* because Randall Flagg kind of peters away to nothing. But to me, the ultimate thing about evil is that it leads nowhere. . . . You can laugh evil out of existence."[53]

However, Flagg isn't laughed out of existence—in the end he reappears in a new location, prepared to wreak havoc on a different group of victims, a scene that was cut from the version of the novel that was published in 1978. King's implication is that evil is always present in the human capacity to do evil. Randall Flagg is "minor league compared to what I assume the devil to be in Christian theology . . . Evil has no power of its own, you know, except for the power people give it. The image I had of Flagg was of a gigantic evil who will begin to deflate . . . I think that if in the end I could have made him into a sort

left KING POSES AT NEW YORK'S PLANET HOLLYWOOD ON JUNE 9, 1994, WITH A MOVIE PROP DEPICTING RANDALL FLAGG FROM THE STAND.

CAPTAIN TRIPS

One name given to the superflu on the West Coast in *The Stand* is "Captain Trips," which King also used as a killer virus in the short story "Night Surf."

"Captain Trips" was a nickname given to Jerry Garcia from the rock group the Grateful Dead because of his fondness for LSD. The Dead were famous for their extensive tours, which provided King with a good analogy for the way the virus spread from person to person across America.

Over the years, many readers have reported coming down with colds or experiencing flu-like symptoms while reading *The Stand*.

invested less time, he might have abandoned it. "There were times when I actively hated *The Stand*, but there was never a time when I did not feel compelled to go on with it. Even when things were going bad with my guys in Boulder, there was a crazy, joyful feeling about the book."[57]

He started taking long walks ("a habit which would, two decades later, get me in a lot of trouble"[58]) as he tried to sort out the complex maze of plots and characters. After struggling with this problem for several weeks, the solution came to him. He had depopulated the world, but his book was becoming overcrowded with characters again. Some of them had to go. The explosion in Boulder that claimed the life of Nick Andros and the ensuing death of Harold Lauder kick-started the book. The quest theme was reinvigorated by the decision to send four members of the Free Zone Committee west, without delay or preparation, for a final confrontation between good and evil.

King wrote the rest of the novel in a little over two months, ending up with a massive 1,400-plus-page manuscript. Though he reduced the size somewhat during his own revisions, Doubleday insisted that he cut the manuscript significantly before they would publish it. They believed that the book was going to be too expensive, which would hurt sales. King was presented with two options: Either he could excise 400 pages or someone at Doubleday would.

This was the second time King had been asked to remove material for purely economic reasons. He felt more strongly about this request than when it came up with *The Shining*, but he complied—though Doubleday's demand added to his growing list of grievances with the publisher and probably contributed to his move to a new publishing house for future novels.

of cringing salesman, a guy who's going bald and wearing red pants and white shoes, I would have done it."[54]

Writing this epic novel was hard work for King. "It got to the point where I began describing it to friends as my own little Vietnam, because I kept telling myself that in another hundred pages or so, I would begin to see light at the end of the tunnel," he remembers.[55] Falling back on a familiar baseball metaphor, King says the book "nearly died going into the third turn and heading for home."[56] He simply didn't know what else to write— a profound case of writer's block after 500 pages. If he had

"THERE NEVER WAS A TIME WHEN I DID NOT FEEL COMPELLED TO GO ON WITH IT. EVEN WHEN THINGS WERE GOING BAD WITH MY GUYS IN BOULDER, THERE WAS A CRAZY, JOYFUL FEELING ABOUT THE BOOK."

THE
Park Lane
Hotel   36 CENTRAL PARK SOUTH, NEW YORK, N.Y. 10019 (212) 371-4000

May 22, 1978.

Concerning the copy-edited MS. of <u>The Stand</u>:

1.) When characters drop g's in their dialogue (and in a few cases, when g's are dropped in narration), I have ~~omitted~~ omitted the customary apostrophe which usually denotes the missing letter. I would like to see this convention followed when setting the book in type. Same applies to the short form of "them" — em. Also: rock n roll, and o for the short form of "of" (as in: "Hand me that pad o paper, Nick.")

2.) Instead of U.S. 95 or U.S. 6, etc., please set US, in all cases, as indicated.
(no period(s))

Thank you very much,

Stephen King

> "THERE IS A DIFFERENCE BETWEEN DOING IT UP RIGHT AND JUST BEING DOWNRIGHT VULGAR. SOME OF WHAT WAS LEFT ON THE CUTTING ROOM FLOOR WHEN I TURNED IN THE TRUNCATED VERSION DESERVED TO BE LEFT THERE, AND THERE IT REMAINS."

One of King's ongoing wishes in the coming years was to see the book published in the form he had intended. Rumors of a reissue came and went throughout the 1980s as one deal after another fell apart. Finally, in 1990, Doubleday published the "uncut and expanded" edition of the book, which became the standard version thereafter.

While restoring most of the old material, King expanded some sections and moved the entire plot forward a decade, a point of contention with some fans of the original version since the update introduced a number of anachronisms (for example, a character is paid one dollar for babysitting). However, he was judicious about the expansion: "[T]here is a difference between doing it up right and just being downright vulgar. Some of what was left on the cutting room floor when I turned in the truncated version deserved to be left there, and there it remains."[59]

Doubleday did not have much faith in the prospects for a twelve-year-old novel. King, too, warned readers about what they were purchasing in his preface to the new edition, part of which was meant to be read before potential buyers reached the cash register. "This is not a brand-new, entirely different version of *The Stand*," he wrote. "You will not discover old characters behaving in new ways, nor will the course of the tale branch off at some point from the old narrative."[60]

The unexpurgated edition of *The Stand* debuted at the top of the best-seller list and stayed on the list for months.

STEPHEN KING IN *THE STAND*

Though Stephen King plays the part of Teddy Weizak—the guy who drives Nadine Cross to Mother Abigail's house and who greets Tom Cullen and Stu Redman when they return to Boulder—in *The Stand* miniseries, that's not the part that most appealed to him.

He frequently suggested that he was best suited to play Tom Cullen, the mentally handicapped giant who spells everything M-O-O-N—a character not all that different from one he had already played: Jordy Verill in *Creepshow*.

However, the character he identified with was Harold Lauder. "Harold is a terrible loner, and he's somebody who feels totally rejected by everybody around him, and he feels fat and ugly and unpleasant most of the time . . . And sometimes I used to feel rejected and unpleasant. I can remember that from high school. And of course Harold is sort of a frustrated writer."[61]

The book almost always appears in first or second place in polls asking fans to name their favorite King novel. "There are people out there who would have been perfectly happy had I died in 1978, the people who come to me and say, 'Oh, you never wrote a book as good as *The Stand*.' I usually tell them how depressing it is to hear them say that something you wrote twenty-eight years ago was your best book."[62]

left KING AS TEDDY WEIZAK, HIS EXTENDED CAMEO FROM THE STAND TV MINISERIES (1994).

ENCLOSED

GALLEY PAGE Final galley page from *The Stand*, containing the Author's Note with King's handwritten changes and additions.

MANUSCRIPT PAGES The scene in which Larry Underwood and Rita escape from New York via the Lincoln Tunnel. King has identified this as his favorite scene in the book.

4 WELCOME TO CASTLE ROCK

"IF YOU FEEL LUCKY, MISTER, SPIN THE WHEEL OF FORTUNE."

THE DEAD ZONE

The Shining and The Stand both end with characters moving to Maine. In the former, Wendy and Danny Torrance meet up with Dick Halloran at the Red Arrow Lodge in western Maine. In the latter, Franny Goldsmith and Stu Redman decide to raise their son Peter in Ogunquit after a short tour of the state, including the town of Castle Rock.

In the summer of 1975, while King was still working on the first draft of The Stand, he and his family moved back to Maine. He didn't feel like he belonged in Boulder, and he recognized that the characters in his Colorado-based novels all had a Maine working-class sensibility.

After finishing The Stand and the novella Rita Hayworth and Shawshank Redemption, he struggled to complete another novel, abandoning two before starting a book about a killer in a small town. "The germ of The Dead Zone never really made it into the novel. . . . I wanted to write about a high school teacher, because that was a profession I knew quite well but I had never used in a novel. I saw him giving an examination to his class—it becomes very quiet, everyone's head is bent over their papers, and a girl comes up and hands him the test. Their hands touch, and he says into this quiet: 'You must go home at once, your house is on fire.' And I could see everyone in the room looking at him—all the eyes, staring."[63]

above KING GOOFING AROUND AT HIS DESK AT THE HAMPDEN ACADEMY, A PUBLIC HIGH SCHOOL IN MAINE WHERE HE STARTED TEACHING ENGLISH IN 1971.

King in his office in Bridgton, Maine, winter 1977.

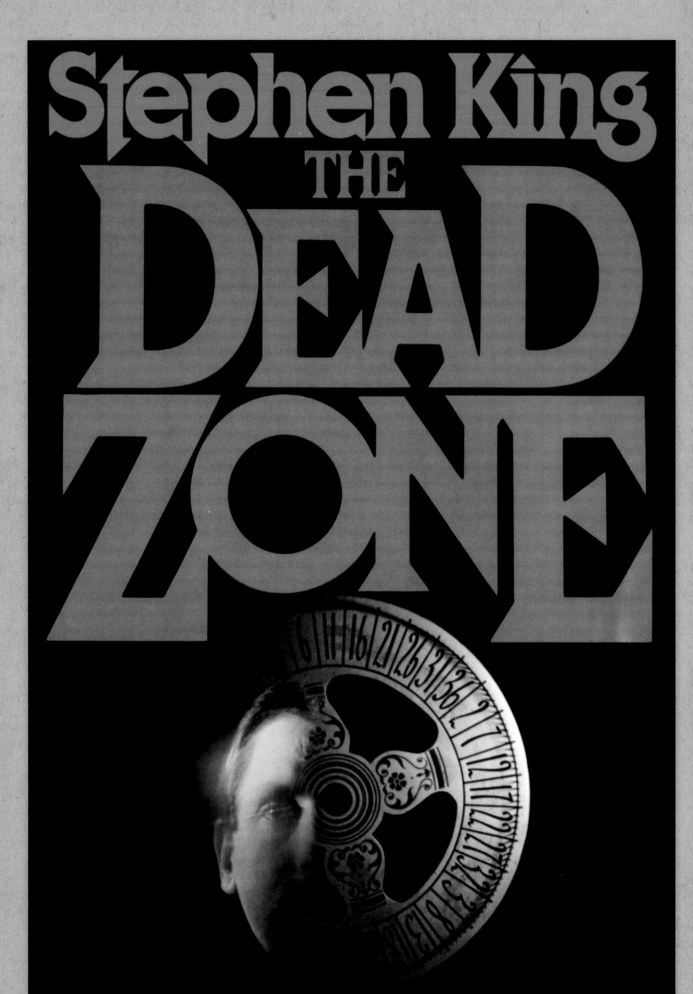

When that book didn't work well either, King put the manuscript aside and began *Firestarter*. "I felt slightly desperate to finish something, and I think that, subconsciously, I returned to what I had written before."[64] Concerned that he was simply reworking *Carrie*, he went back to *The Dead Zone*, completing the novel in 1977.

King reminisces about how the main character's affliction developed in his mind: "Little by little [Johnny Smith's ability] refined itself into this psychic talent that's known as 'prolepsis.'. . . It's the ability to be sort of a human bloodhound—to touch objects and get visions from them. . . Everybody would sort of shun him as a result of this. Everybody would be afraid of him . . . I went back a little further and began to ask myself all these other questions about what would happen if you could really see the future. The more I wrote, the more it seemed like just a really horrible thing, you know? People wouldn't like you."[65]

King's relocation to Maine was only one of several transitions in his life. For the first time he engaged the services of a literary agent, and he severed his association with Doubleday. Kirby McCauley negotiated a $2.5-million advance with New American Library for three novels: *The Dead Zone*, *Firestarter*, and another unspecified book—a vast improvement over the paltry advances King had received in the past. This deal also meant he would no longer have to split the lucrative paperback rights with the publisher.

The Dead Zone is set in Cleaves Mills, Maine, a small town close to Castle Rock, one of King's most famous fictional

left VIKING PRESS HARDCOVER EDITION OF THE DEAD ZONE. above A DRIVE-IN MARQUEE IN INDIANAPOLIS, ANNOUNCING A KING MOVIE MARATHON IN 1984.

KING WAS KNOCKED UNCONSCIOUS BY A HOCKEY PLAYER WHEN HE WAS FOUR, AN INCIDENT THAT FOUND ITS WAY INTO THE DEAD ZONE.

locations, which appears in this book for the first time. The two towns are modeled after Durham and Lisbon Falls, where King grew up and attended high school. The name Castle Rock is taken from William Golding's novel *Lord of the Flies*, which had a major influence on King's work.

The main character, Johnny Smith, acquires his psychic abilities after two accidents. The first takes place on a frozen pond when he is six. An older boy accidentally knocks him down and his head hits the ice. He has a precognitive episode when he regains consciousness, though no one—not even Johnny—realizes it. The accident was drawn from King's life: "It's one of the earliest things I can remember: being hit by a hockey player, knocked out, and coming to about five minutes later. I was probably no more than four years old. It's one of those things you grab hold of and put in a book because it fits."[66]

The second incident happens when Johnny is twenty-three. He's a teacher at Cleaves Mills High School, and has a girlfriend he will probably marry. Everything seems to be going his way. Heading home after a date, he is involved in a car accident that leaves him in a coma for five years.

Though King's previous novels featured evil personified—vampires, the ghosts in a haunted hotel, the diabolical Randall Flagg—the evil in *The Dead Zone* is more abstract. What happens to Johnny is a seemingly random act of fate, foreshadowed by his run of luck at the Wheel of Fortune at the fair during his date with Sarah Bracknell. His decision to not spend the night with Sarah after eating a bad hot dog put him on a collision course with fate.

"IT SEEMS AS THOUGH OUR LIVES ARE GOVERNED BY THESE LITTLE 'CHANCE' EVENTS. IF YOU DRAW BACK AND TAKE A LONGER VIEW, MAYBE THERE'S A PATTERN TO IT ALL."

THE CORRUPTING POWER OF RELIGION

A theme that comes up often in King's novels is the power of religion over vulnerable people, primarily matronly women. Johnny Smith's mother, Vera, falls prey to zealots who believe in psychic phenomena. King says that he doesn't have anything against religion, "because most people see it as the means to another world and have a good handle on it. Vera Smith . . . has gone one step beyond that. She's not over the line into religious mania the way that Carrie White's mother is, but at the same time she's supplanting the Bible and the power of God with a lot of what I think of as pagan stuff."[67]

Other characters cut from the same cloth include Mrs. Carmody from *The Mist* and Sylvia Pittston from *The Gunslinger*. "I see a correlation between the religious idea and the psychic idea because they are both a sort of struggle for power by people who are powerless. A lot of times, the people who are real fanatical believers in psychic phenomena are people like Vera Smith. Sometimes fundamentalism and the belief in the psychic cross."[68]

PIPER LAURIE, HOLDING HER DAUGHTER (SISSY SPACEK), IN HER OSCAR-NOMINATED ROLE AS MARGARET WHITE IN <u>CARRIE</u>, 1976.

King explains, "To me, everything that's symbolic in *The Dead Zone* points in one direction. It seems as though our lives are governed by these little 'chance' events. If you draw back and take a longer view, maybe there's a pattern to it all. I like to think there is; I'd hate to think that life is all random."[69]

Johnny emerges from his coma like Rip Van Winkle to discover that his twenties have been stolen from him. His mother is dead; his girlfriend is married to another man and has a son. His memories are full of "dead zones," things he can't recall. To make matters worse, he has visions of the future, and most of them aren't pleasant.

The media are drawn to Johnny's story. He becomes a minor celebrity, and people start demanding that he help them. Tabloid journalists stalk him. When he realizes that he can't satisfy all of their requests, he withdraws from society. It is tempting to think that King was reflecting on the difficulties he was having adjusting to his own loss of privacy as a result of his newfound celebrity—by this point strangers were constantly contacting

him with requests for autographs, money, or contacts in the publishing industry.

Johnny reluctantly accepts one plea for assistance. He agrees to help Sheriff Bannerman solve a series of murders in nearby Castle Rock and quickly identifies one of Bannerman's deputies, Frank Dodd, as the killer. There's nothing supernatural about Dodd's murders, although his spirit would later be invoked as the monster who haunts Castle Rock in *Cujo*—the book where Sheriff Bannerman meets his demise at the jaws of a rabid Saint Bernard. Dodd becomes the bogeyman who inhabits Tad Trenton's closet.

The Dead Zone gets down to its primary business, however, when it tackles the subject of Greg Stillson, the unscrupulous politician who, when he was a Bible salesman, kicked a dog to death and who will—according to Johnny's visions—one day occupy the Oval Office and precipitate a full-scale nuclear war. By this point, Johnny has enough of a track record with his vision to trust what he foresees. He is presented with a moral conundrum: Is he obligated to take action to prevent this future

left KING, WEARING A T-SHIRT FROM THE FILM VERSION OF THE DEAD ZONE, SIGNS A MOVIE POSTER FOR A FAN, CIRCA 1985.
above MEMORABILIA FROM KING'S OFFICE, INCLUDING AN ANTI-VAMPIRE KIT, A SET PHOTO FROM CREEPSHOW, AND A BEST-SELLER LIST WITH FIRESTARTER AND THE DEAD ZONE SITTING ATOP OF THE HARDCOVER AND PAPERBACK LISTS RESPECTIVELY.

catastrophe, and, if he carries out his plan to kill Stillson, are his actions justified?

King posits, "*The Dead Zone* arose from two questions: Can a political assassin ever be right? And if he is, could you make him the protagonist of a novel?"[70] Or, in other words, "Would you kill Hitler if you could go back in a time machine?"[71] Readers have the benefit of insight into Stillson's true nature, details of his corrupt activities that are not available to most of the book's characters. King uses this to generate support for Johnny's actions—he does indeed become a sympathetic assassin. He happens to be the only person who can see through Stillson's façade. King says, "Johnny is different from other violent, paranoid mystics in only one way: He really *can* see the future. Only don't they all say that?"[72]

He casts Johnny as a genuinely decent guy—his name is the epitome of average—and ultimately shies away from having Johnny kill Stillson. "Part of me said, You don't want to do this because if he kills Greg Stillson in the book, and ten years from now somebody knocks off President Anderson or President Carter, and they ask him, 'Why did you do it?' The guy says, 'I got the idea from Stephen King's novel *The Dead Zone*,' I would have to quietly pack my bags and move to Costa Rica.

So I was ambivalent. A lot of me wanted to kill [Stillson] and felt the ending was something of a cop-out."[73]

King calls *The Dead Zone* "plot-driven," meaning that the characters of his protagonist and antagonist were determined by the story he wanted to tell.[74] It remains one of his personal favorites. Thanks in part to an attractively designed book cover and an aggressive marketing campaign, *The Dead Zone* became King's first number-one hardcover best-seller, and it stayed on the list for nearly half a year. Another book that came out a month earlier, *The Long Walk*, published under his pen name Richard Bachman, vanished from shelves shortly after it was released.

After he finished *The Dead Zone*, the Kings moved to Fleet in Hampshire, England, where they planned to stay for a year, during which time King hoped to absorb enough of the landscape to write a book set there. However, the only story inspired by the trip was "Crouch End," which he wrote after getting lost on the way to visit Peter Straub's home in the village of the same name. The two authors agreed at the time to collaborate on a novel, *The Talisman*, written several years later.

During their stay in England, King completed *Cujo,* but after only three months, the family returned to Maine.

above KING MEETS WITH U.S. CONGRESSMAN JOHN BALDACCI AND PRESIDENT BILL CLINTON, CIRCA 1996.

ZONE RADIO

The car King rented at Logan Airport in Boston to get back to Bangor had only an AM radio. During the four-hour drive, he twisted the dial constantly, but all he could find were talk shows, sports, news, religious programs, and trading post call-in shows. No rock music.

With the advent of stereo broadcasting, FM had become the home of rock and roll. "But it wasn't *my* rock and roll; not the kind I grew up with, where screaming hipster jocks like Arnie Ginsberg and Cousin Brucie made you laugh and then blew your socks off."[75]

He decided to do something about it. On Halloween Day in 1983, he purchased WACZ, which until recently had been WLBZ, operating since the 1920s, and rechristened it WZON after *The Dead Zone*.

The station was never a financial success, but it had one clear benefit for someone who listens to rock music while writing—King always knew where to turn the dial to find what he wanted while working.

After converting to a commercial-free format in 1988, King sold his radio license in 1990. He repurchased it again in 1993 after the station switched to a talk-radio format and then went bankrupt. The Zone Corporation now owns and operates three Maine stations, WZON (The Sports Zone), WKIT (Brewer's Rock N Roll Zone), and WDME (Dover-Foxcroft, from the Woods of Maine). WZON, an ESPN affiliate, broadcasts primarily local sports, but ensures that every Boston Red Sox game is aired in Maine.

1980s LOGO AND BUMPER STICKER FOR KING'S RADIO STATION, WZON.

BRITISH PAPERBACK EDITION OF THE
DEAD ZONE, PUBLISHED BY FUTURA.

ENCLOSED

COPYEDITS A copyedited page of *The Dead Zone*'s prologue. King was apparently still making significant changes to the manuscript at this point, too, and some of the copy editor's deletions (e.g., two instances of the word "from" in the opening paragraph) were rejected by King and appear in the final version of the book.

MANUSCRIPT Page from King's first draft of *The Dead Zone*. Note that this page is designated as "1," so the prologue must have been a later addition to the novel.

HANDWRITTEN DRAFT Four hand-written pages of the first draft of *Cujo*. The final version of the novel has only a few changes compared to this manuscript; most notably, a few sentences are inserted into the paragraph at the top of page 88.

KING IN HIS HOME OFFICE IN BRIDGTON, MAINE, CIRCA JANUARY 1977.

5 SOMETIMES DEAD IS BETTER

"IN THE TEXTURE OF THOSE RUDE MARKERS WERE TRUTHS WHICH EVEN A CHILD'S HANDS COULD FEEL."

PET SEMATARY

In 1978, King was invited to be writer-in-residence at the English department of his alma mater, the University of Maine, which is located in Orono, a few miles from Bangor. King agreed, partly to thank the university for its support of him as a young writer. Among the classes he taught were Introduction to Creative Writing and a course on the literature of the fantastic, the notes from which would become the starting point for *Danse Macabre*.

During his tenure at the university, King moved his family into a rented house on a major highway in Orrington. The heavy traffic included transports heading to and from a nearby chemical plant. A new neighbor warned the Kings to keep their pets away from the road, which, she said, had "used up a lot of animals."[76]

In support of this claim, the Kings discovered a burial ground not far from the house, with PETS SEMATARY written on a sign in a childish hand. Among its residents: dogs, cats, birds, and a goat.

Shortly after they moved in, King's daughter Naomi's cat Smucky was found dead on the side of the road when they returned from a trip to town. King's first impulse was to tell Naomi that the cat had wandered away. His wife, however, believed this was an opportunity to teach a life lesson. They broke the news to their daughter and conducted a feline funeral, committing Smucky's mortal remains to the pet cemetery. A few nights later, King discovered Naomi in the garage, jumping up and down on sheets of bubble wrap, indignant over the loss of her pet. "He was *my* cat. Let God have his own cat," she was repeating.[77]

The road almost "used up" the Kings' youngest son, too. Owen was about eighteen months old when he wandered dangerously close to the highway. To this day, King isn't sure whether he knocked his son down before he reached the highway as one of the tankers approached or whether Owen tripped over his own feet. Owen had been born with an unusually large head, and the Kings had already agonized over the possibility that they might lose him to hydrocephalus. This near miss was an unwelcome reminder of the fragility of their children.

Even someone who isn't a writer would obsess over the other possible outcomes of that incident, the "what ifs" that drive the creative impulse. King felt compelled to explore the aftermath of such a death, working in a room in the store

right A PET IN A CEMETERY: KING AND ONE OF NEARLY TWENTY CATS WHO PLAYED THE GENERAL IN THE MOVIE CAT'S EYE.

MT. HOPE CEMETERY IN BANGOR, MAINE, USED DURING THE FILMING OF <u>PET SEMATARY</u>. BOTH THE LARGEST HEADSTONE AND THE ONE ON THE RIGHT ARE INSCRIBED WITH THE FAMILY NAME KING, THOUGH UNRELATED TO THE AUTHOR.

across the street from their house. Naomi's reaction to the death of her cat and Owen's misadventure both made it into the book.

In the middle of 1979, six weeks after he finished writing *Pet Sematary*, King reread the novel and deemed it too gruesome and disturbing to be published. His wife found the scene where two-year-old Gage Creed dies hard to deal with. Taking her advice, and that of his friend and fellow novelist Peter Straub, he put the manuscript in a drawer, where he intended for it to stay forever, and moved on to *The Dead Zone*.

Since he is occasionally unguarded with interviewers, King mentioned the book in passing in response to a question about whether he had ever written anything too terrible to be published. A mythos arose around the novel.

Pet Sematary would have remained in the drawer, though, if not for an ongoing struggle with Doubleday. The contract he

had signed with his original publisher contained a clause that allowed them to mete out his accrued royalties at a rate of only $50,000 per year, while investing the rest. This practice allowed authors to defer taxes on this money. No one—including King—could have anticipated how quickly his investment account would grow. By the early 1980s, Doubleday had millions of his dollars in reserve, and it would have taken the rest of his life for it to be doled out at the specified rate.

An agreement was reached to cancel the clause in the contract. If King allowed them to publish another novel, Doubleday would release his accrued money. However, the only manuscript available was *Pet Sematary*. After making sure his wife didn't object, he agreed to give them the manuscript. Because of his strong feelings about the novel, though, he refused to assist the publisher in promoting it and rarely talked about it in interviews in subsequent years.

above THE SIGN AT THE ORIGINAL "PETS SEMATARY," LOCATED NEAR THE HOUSE KING RENTED IN ORRINGTON WHILE WRITER-IN-RESIDENCE AT THE UNIVERSITY OF MAINE.

"THE REASON YOU GROW TO LOVE THEM IS BECAUSE I LOVED THEM. AND THEN IT ALL FALLS DOWN."

Physician Louis Creed has just moved with his family (wife Rachel, young children Ellie and Gage) to the University of Maine. This nuclear family, one of the most well adjusted in King's novels (despite Rachel's father's disapproval of the marriage because Louis isn't Jewish), moves into a house in Ludlow very much like the one the Kings occupied in Orrington, with its busy highway out front and a pet cemetery nearby. King says, "That's what's so awful about *Pet Sematary*, why it's such a dreadful book, because you're welcomed into this family. It's a domestic drama. It's Mommy and Daddy and the little daughter and the baby son. The reason you grow to love them is that I loved them. And then it all falls down. And people say, 'Well, how could you do that?'"[78]

Louis thinks death is "except perhaps for childbirth, the most natural thing in the world." It isn't a distant prospect—"we're all close, all the time," he tells his wife. As a doctor, he sees himself as somewhat above the laws of nature, though, because it is occasionally within his power to prevent death. However, he doesn't believe in an afterlife. "He had been present at many deathbeds and had never felt a soul bullet pass him on its way to . . . wherever." This includes the soul of Victor Pascow, the student struck by a car on Louis's first day of work, who delivered an ominous warning about the pet cemetery moments before he died.

The nearby animal burial ground motivates a discussion of death with Ellie, who is distraught when she realizes that her cat, Church, might die someday. Rachel is offended by the

above THIS ROAD, ROUTE 15 IN ORRINGTON, MAINE, HAS "USED UP A LOT OF PETS." THE SCENE WHERE GAGE CREED IS KILLED IN PET SEMATARY WAS FILMED HERE. right CHURCH THE CAT RETURNS TO LIFE IN THIS SCENE FROM THE MOVIE ADAPTATION OF PET SEMATARY.

THE MONKEY'S PAW

Though famous in his lifetime for his humorous writings, W. W. Jacobs is now remembered best for the horror story "The Monkey's Paw" (1902). This tale uses the classic idea of being granted three wishes, but warns that there may be dire consequences for using the talisman. The monkey's paw that Sergeant-Major Morris shows to the main character, Mr. White, "had a spell put on it by an old fakir, a very holy man. He wanted to show that fate ruled people's lives, and that those who interfered with it did so to their sorrow."

Morris doesn't say how he used his own three wishes, but he does reveal that the man who possessed the monkey's paw before him used his last wish to ask for death. Just as he is about to give it to White, Morris instead throws the paw into the fire and urges White to let it burn. White can't permit that, though. The temptation is too great—he even forces Morris to accept some trifle in compensation.

White's first wish is for money: 200 pounds. The monkey's paw writhes in his hand. A short while later, a stranger arrives to deliver the sad news that their only child, Herbert, has been killed in an industrial accident. The emissary hands over a check—for 200 pounds.

After the funeral, Mrs. White forces her husband to make a second wish: to bring back their son. Time passes—exactly the amount of time it would take for Herbert to stagger two miles from the graveyard down the road to their house. Mr. White realizes the nature of the disfigured monster he has summoned and makes a final wish as his wife is about to open the door. Then, a "cold wind rushed up the staircase, and a long loud wail of disappointment and misery from his wife gave him courage to run down to her side, and then to the gate beyond. The street lamp flickering opposite shone on a quiet and deserted road."

King uses an excerpt from this story as an epigraph for Part III of *Pet Sematary*. He still had the story in mind when writing *The Dead Zone*. Johnny Smith's physician tracks down his mother, long presumed dead, based on Johnny's vision, but hangs up when she comes to the phone. Johnny remembers the Jacobs story and agrees with the doctor's decision: "Maybe some things were better lost than found."

pet cemetery, calling it a "tourist attraction." She has a death phobia—her sister suffered horribly with spinal meningitis, and Rachel was alone with her on the day she died. The incident scarred her, and Louis learned early in their marriage to tread carefully around the topic of death.

Rachel and the kids are visiting her parents when Church is killed. Unlike Herbert Smith in "The Monkey's Paw," the W. W. Jacobs story that inspired King, Church isn't mangled or disfigured. Louis follows the path that King wasn't allowed to take—he plans to bury his daughter's pet and pretend that Church has simply wandered off. He's sparing Ellie's feelings, but he's also avoiding Rachel's refusal to deal with death.

Louis's elderly neighbor, Jud Crandall, plays the part of Sergeant-Major Morris from "The Monkey's Paw." Louis saved Jud's wife, Norma, after a massive heart attack, so Jud repays the debt by leading Louis to a forsaken Micmac burial ground beyond the pet cemetery, where the earth is stony and hard and, according to tradition, each man must bury his own. The Micmacs abandoned the land after a mythical creature known as a Wendigo invaded it. Jud buried his own dog, Spot, there when he was ten. Louis doesn't appreciate the significance of the fact that the cairns built over the existing graves have all fallen over.

Church comes back the next afternoon, looking much the same as before but now graceless and smelling of sour earth and death, no matter how many times he's washed. He doesn't purr anymore, either. King makes a passing reference to a classic monster constructed out of dead parts when Louis calls Church "Frankencat."

Jud justifies his actions—even though he knows that the animals that come back from the burial ground are fundamentally changed—by saying that "kids need to know that sometimes dead is better." He feels it's a lesson Ellie—and perhaps Rachel as well—needs to learn. However, that isn't the real reason Jud takes Louis on the strange expedition through the woods. The burial ground was a long-guarded secret that he felt compelled to share with someone else.

Norma Crandall's subsequent death provides King with the chance to explore a topic of interest to him—burial practices and customs. Louis offers moral support while Jud makes the arrangements for Norma's funeral. Louis's uncle was employed in the "quiet trade," his term for the work of morticians, so he knows about embalming, whether the deceased's hair will be washed and all the other questions people don't ponder until confronted with death.

Through Louis's discussion with Ellie about Norma's funeral, King scrutinizes some of the rituals—why people drive with their headlights on during the funeral procession, for example. Ellie, now almost six, is much more curious and less emotional about the subject than she had been almost a year earlier. She even thinks she could "take it" if Church died. When she learns that her father will be a pallbearer, she offers a piece of sage advice: "Don't drop her."

Pet Sematary is a dark novel, but it becomes relentlessly bleak the moment King recreates the incident that inspired the

above PUBLICITY PHOTO BY THOMAS VICTOR, ISSUED BY VIKING PRESS IN 1986.

book. As if unwilling to drop such a bombshell on his readers through narrative of the fateful events that led up to Gage's death, King begins the book's second section with Louis talking about his son's funeral, after foreshadowing that something dire is about to happen at the end of the previous section by discussing the last happy day of Louis's life.

Gage's death devastates the family. Ellie rails at God, using the biblical story of Lazarus as evidence that God could "take it back" if he chose to do so. Louis is so blindsided that his mind turns to the Micmac burial ground, despite Jud's warning not to be curious about such matters. He begins to rationalize. Church came back, changed and distasteful, true, but at least they all have relationships with the cat. The reader is in lockstep with Louis as he talks himself into doing the unthinkable.

Jud realizes what Louis is considering and tells him about Timmy Baterman, the one known case where a person was buried in the ancient grounds, to dissuade him. The reincarnated Baterman was a sly and crafty zombie who knew terrible secrets about people.

After taking his readers through the grim events of Gage's visitation, including a struggle between Louis and his father-in-law that nearly knocks over Gage's coffin, King pretends that none of this happened. However, Louis's dream that everything is all right, tracing forward the arc of Gage's successful life into adulthood, is the only moment in the final third of the novel with any hint of optimism. It's the writer's "what if" cast in a different direction.

What follows is one of the most discomforting and harrowing passages in all of King's fiction. Louis sends the remains of his family back to Chicago to stay with Rachel's parents while he puts his misguided plan into effect. Intellectually, he accepts that Jud's story about Baterman might be true and that he might have to kill Gage if he comes back altered. However, he's also planning the family's escape to a new location if Gage comes back normal. They wouldn't be able to live in Ludlow anymore with a resurrected son, after all.

The final vector in this family tragedy is initiated by Ellie, who has mild precognition. She dreams about Gage's coffin being empty and about Victor Pascow, the student who died on Louis's first day at work. When Rachel hears this, she reverses course and returns alone to Maine. King says that Rachel made that decision on her own: "I didn't make her come back, I didn't say she would come back. She just ran back. Because characters get away sometimes and they start to go on their own and all you can do is hope that they go in a place that won't make the book too uncomfortable for you."[79]

The police almost catch Louis in the act of disinterring his son's body. In a gruesome touch of realism, Louis thinks his son's head is missing only to discover that moss has grown on the corpse after his burial. However, even the appearance of the massive Wendigo in the dark woods doesn't deter him from his path. It's as if the forces that lurk beneath the surface of the burial ground want Gage's soul as much as the Overlook Hotel wanted Danny Torrance, feeding off the survivors' grief and finding ways to keep the cycle going.

Gage returns as a homicidal monster. His first victim is Jud Crandall. The evil entity inhabiting his little body—still clad in his burial suit—has a score to settle with Jud for meddling in the past. Next comes Gage's mother, who shows up at the most inopportune moment.

Rachel's death drives Louis beyond the brink of sanity. Rationalization kicks in again—he itemizes all the reasons why things went wrong with Gage and how things might work better for his freshly deceased wife. Unlike Mr. White in "The Monkey's Paw," Louis hasn't learned his lesson. He doesn't wish away the abominations he has helped create. Instead, he makes one last trip to the burial ground and then waits for Rachel to return.

WENDIGO

Several Native American cultures believed in the Wendigo, a giant creature with glowing eyes. Wendigos are associated with cannibalism, which some early communities resorted to during the harsh winters of the northeastern United States and Canada.

Most tribes felt that the proper response to starvation was to commit suicide rather than give in to the temptation of cannibalism. In *Pet Sematary*, Jud Crandall claims that the natives concocted the Wendigo myth to absolve themselves of guilt for this taboo, placing the blame instead on a creature whose touch gave rise to the craving for human flesh.

According to legend, Wendigos were voracious, insatiable creatures. Every time they consumed people to sate their hunger, they grew larger, which made them even more emaciated than before. People who were overcome by greed could become a Wendigo in some belief systems.

In his 1910 short story "The Wendigo," Algernon Blackwood describes the creature as "the Call of the Wild personified, which some natures hear to their own destruction."[80]

The last line of the novel is one of the most devastating in King's works. Rachel's hand is cold and her voice is gravelly as she says, "Darling." The speaker of this word is identified as "it" rather than "she."

What happens next is left as an exercise for the reader.

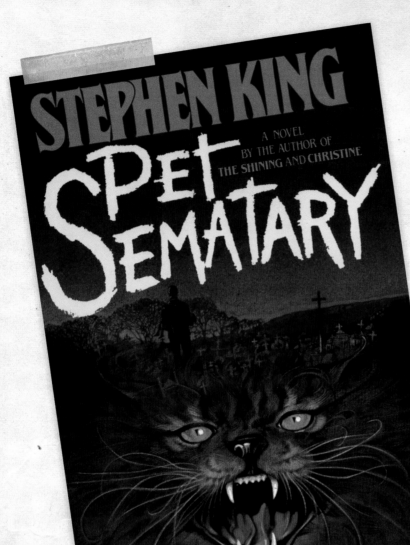

DOUBLEDAY HARDCOVER EDITION OF PET SEMATARY.

ENCLOSED

MANUSCRIPT In these pages from *Pet Sematary*, Louis dreams of being guided through the burial ground by Victor Pascow, the student who died on Louis's first day of work. King made a note to himself on the back of one of the pages and struggled over the names of certain bones. One of the editors caught a continuity error concerning Louis and Rachel's sleeping arrangements.

STEPHEN KING
Friedhof der Kuscheltiere
ROMAN

German edition of Pet Sematary, published by Bertelsmann. The title translates roughly to "Cemetery for Stuffed Animals."

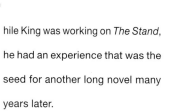

6 PENNYWISE LIVES

"REMEMBER THE SIMPLEST THING OF ALL—
HOW IT IS TO BE CHILDREN, SECURE IN BELIEF
AND THUS AFRAID OF THE DARK."

IT

While King was working on *The Stand*, he had an experience that was the seed for another long novel many years later.

In Boulder, the family vehicle was an AMC Matador, "an admirable car right up until the day when its transmission just fell out onto Pearl Street."[81] Two days after the car was towed to a dealership on the east end of the city, King received word that it was ready to be picked up.

Rather than call a cab, King decided he needed the exercise and walked the three miles to the dealership, eventually ending up on a narrow unlit road at twilight. He recalls the moment vividly: "I was aware of how alone I was. About a quarter of a mile along this road was a wooden bridge, humped and oddly quaint, spanning a stream. I walked across it. I was wearing cowboy boots with rundown heels, and I was very aware of the sound they made on the boards; they sounded like a hollow clock.[82]

"I suppose I should have thought of Randall Flagg, since I was all wrapped up in his life just then, but instead I thought of the story of Billy Goats Gruff, the troll who says, 'Who's that trip-trapping on my bridge?' and the whole story just bounced into my mind on a pogo-stick. Not the characters, but the split time-frame, the accelerated bounces that would end with a complete breakdown, which might result in a feeling of 'no time,' all the monsters that were one monster . . . the troll under the bridge, of course."[83]

This wasn't the first time the idea of an underground monster had occurred to King. His juvenile story "The Thing at the Bottom of the Well" from *People, Places & Things*, written in the early 1960s, features a subterranean creature that loves to torture animals and people.

While King worked on other projects over the next two years, the image of the troll returned to him. He saw the bridge as a symbol for transition—though the idea of writing with symbolism in mind troubled him, as did the possibility that some sort of theme was attached.

The book that developed from these notions is *It*, which King thought of at the time as his magnum opus and the end of a phase—the last book he intended to write about supernatural monsters and kids in jeopardy. "The book is the summation of everything I have done and learned in my whole life to this point,"[84] he said. "Every monster that ever lived is in this book. This is it, this is the final exam."[85]

right TIM CURRY AS PENNYWISE THE CLOWN, THE MOST FAMILIAR FORM OF THE MONSTER FROM IT, IN A STILL FROM THE 1990 TV MINISERIES.

The Kenduskeag Stream canal passing through downtown Bangor. The murder of Charles O. Howard in July 1984 inspired King to write a similar scene in _It_ involving Adrian Mellon.

Chris, Rex, Dave, David H, Andy, Dean, Brian, Duncan, Dana, Steve, Jamie

"THE IDEA IS TO COME BACK AND CONFRONT YOUR CHILDHOOD, IN A SENSE RELIVE IT IF YOU CAN, SO THAT YOU CAN BE WHOLE."

King says that he wrote about children for so many years because he had small children of his own.[86] He believes that a person can't truly finish with his childhood until his offspring have finished with theirs: "You get a kind of perspective on what your own childhood meant, what you went through."[87] "I'm interested in the notion of finishing off one's childhood as one completes making a wheel," he said in an interview. "The idea is to come back and confront your childhood, in a sense relive it if you can, so that you can be whole."[88]

It is an extension of his novella *The Body*. Both stories feature children growing up in Maine in the 1950s, navigating the harrowing path from innocence to adulthood. The book moves smoothly back and forth between two eras—the 1950s of King's youth, and the 1980s, when he was reflecting on that time as an adult. The stories of the seven friends, outsiders who make up the self-anointed Losers' Club, move in parallel, alternating faster as they reach individual climaxes that are almost exact copies of one another except for the ages of the characters.

"When I started to work on *It* . . . I realized that I was writing about the way we use our imaginations at different points in our lives."[89] King postulates that children are better capable of withstanding the creature they call Pennywise because their developing minds have not yet excluded the possibility of a monster that manifests itself differently to everyone who sees it—werewolf, mummy, giant pterodactyl—feeding on the innate fears that haunt the child's mind. "Kids live in a constant state of shock," he suggests.[90]

above A GROUP SHOT OF KING WITH HIS CHILDHOOD FRIENDS, CIRCA JUNE 1960. KING IS IN THE BACK ROW, FAR RIGHT.

Pennywise knows that adults have a disadvantage against him because they have lost much of their imagination and sense of wonder at the world. After the members of the Losers' Club injure the monster, it decides to let them go and deal with them during its next cycle of strength when they are adults.

The book also explores how childhood memories grow vague with time. By 1985, when the grown-up Losers reassemble in the fictional city of Derry, they recall little from 1958. Only Mike Hanlon, who has remained in the city and has been keeping notes about those long-ago events, remembers anything. At the beginning of *On Writing*, King confesses that his own childhood "is a fogged-out landscape from which occasional memories appear like isolated trees . . . the kind that look as if they might like to grab and eat you." However, while writing *It*, he says he entered a kind of semi-dreaming state that opened his mind to a lot of his memories.[91]

The 1958 "childhood" version of Derry is modeled after Stratford, Connecticut, where King lived for a time as a child before moving to Maine. That was where he discovered the barrens—the forsaken place where the Losers play. King's older

brother, Dave, showed him how to dam the stream, and a cop very much like Mr. Nell appeared after the brothers flooded the neighborhood. The Derry Public Library where Mike Hanlon works is based on the library King frequented in Stratford, and the corridor separating the adult section from the children's section represents another kind of bridge, a symbol of the transition between childhood and adulthood.

However, the 1985 version of Derry—the city the former Losers return to as adults—is grim, dark, and unforgiving. Behind its closed doors, spouses abuse each other and their children. There is rampant racism, homophobia, prejudice, and general intolerance of outsiders. Even without Pennywise feeding on and stoking its fears, it is an unlovely place.

The most familiar form of Pennywise—the evil clown— came to King while he was walking in downtown Bangor after a heavy rainstorm. He wondered whether an entire city could be haunted. Hearkening back to the story of the Billy Goats Gruff, he visualized Bangor as a metaphor for the bridge: "The water was going down the gutter and running down the sewers. As I looked at this one sewer as I was going by, the voice inside

above THE STRATFORD, CONNECTICUT, PUBLIC LIBRARY, CIRCA 1896. THE LIBRARY WAS THE INSPIRATION FOR THE DERRY PUBLIC LIBRARY IN IT.

THE STEPHEN KING TOUR OF BANGOR

Since Bangor hosts a sizeable number of pilgrims who travel to the city to see Stephen King's house and locations from his novels, the Greater Bangor Convention and Visitors Bureau offers a themed bus tour several times each summer.

Among the destinations seen on the tour are the Standpipe, the Paul Bunyan statue, Mount Hope Cemetery (used during the filming of *Pet Sematary*), and Bangor's version of the barrens. Other stops include sites from King's past, among them the laundry where he worked after college and some of his early residences, as well as places that the Kings' generosity helped construct or expand, like the community swimming pool, the baseball field at Mansfield Park, and the Bangor Public Library.

The highlight of the tour is King's home, with its wrought iron fence featuring bats, spiders, and other intricate design elements. Out of respect for the family's privacy, the bus doesn't stop at the house, and the tour operators have an agreement with the Kings to ensure that they won't drive by their house too often.

BANGOR IS THE BIRTHPLACE OF THE FOLK ICON PAUL BUNYAN. STANDING OVER THIRTY FEET TALL, THIS STATUE WAS DESIGNED BY A LOCAL ARTIST AND DONATED TO THE CITY IN 1959.

RICHARD BACHMAN, PAPERBACK WRITER

Richard Bachman wasn't King's first choice for a pseudonym. When he submitted a novel called *Getting It On*, the pen name he chose was Guy Pillsbury, his grandfather's name. However, his cover was blown internally at the publisher, so he was pressed to come up with a new alias in short order. "There was a novel by Richard Stark on my desk so I used the name Richard and that's kind of funny because Richard Stark is in itself a pen name for Donald Westlake, and what was playing on the record player was 'You Ain't Seen Nothin' Yet' by Bachman Turner Overdrive, so I put the two of them together and came up with Richard Bachman."[92]

The book had to get a new title, too—it became *Rage*, the book that Bill Thompson had worked hard to get published during his first interactions with King.

The first four books published by Richard Bachman were issued as paperbacks without fanfare "to fill the drugstore and bus-station racks of America."[93] This was at King's request—he wanted the books to find an audience on their own. They didn't.

When *Thinner* came out in hardcover in 1984, one reviewer declared that this was what Stephen King would write like if Stephen King could write. Others agreed, and the fake author photo and bio on the dust jacket didn't dissuade them. A diligent bookstore employee researched the copyrights for the previous four novels at the Library of Congress, where he found the smoking gun that proved the books were written by King. Sales of *Thinner*, already more impressive than for any of the previous Bachman books, skyrocketed after the news broke.

Richard Bachman died of "cancer of the pseudonym" after his identity was exposed. He left behind a widow, Claudia Inez Bachman. Their only son "died in an unfortunate accident at the age of six (he fell through a well cover and drowned)."[94]

That hasn't stopped "Dicky," however. He has published two posthumous novels to date, *The Regulators* and *Blaze*.

NEW AMERICAN LIBRARY FIRST EDITION OF THINNER, KING'S FIFTH NOVEL PUBLISHED UNDER THE PEN NAME RICHARD BACHMAN—AND THE FIRST IN HARDCOVER.

STEPHEN

KING

IT

VIKING

Author's set

AFTER KING'S PSEUDONYM WAS REVEALED,
VIKING PENGUIN ADDED THE BACHMAN
TITLES TO THE AUTHOR'S AD CARD IN IT,
OPPOSITE THE TITLE PAGE.

ALSO BY STEPHEN KING

5
6
8
9   **NOVELS**
10   Carrie
11   'Salem's Lot
12   The Shining
13   The Stand
14   The Dead Zone
15   Firestarter
16   Cujo
17   The Dark Tower
18   Christine
19   Pet Sematary
20   The Talisman (with Peter Straub)
21
22   **COLLECTIONS**
23   Night Shift
24   Different Seasons
25   Skeleton Crew
26
27   **NONFICTION**
28   Danse Macabre
29
30   **SCREENPLAYS**
31   Creepshow
32   Cat's Eye
           Silver Bullet
           Maximum Overdrive

AS RICHARD BACHMAN
Rage
The Long Walk
Roadwork
The Running Man
Thinner

In the novel It, several children supposedly drowned over the years in the standpipe. In reality, an 11-year-old boy died after falling from a railing of Bangor's Thomas Hill Standpipe in 1940.

speaks up again and says, 'The troll lives there too, only when he's in the sewers he has a clown suit on.'"[95]

In the book, the murder of Adrian Mellon, the first killing to catch adult Mike Hanlon's attention, is based on a real incident in Bangor in 1984. The victim did not drown after being thrown off the bridge into the stream—he suffocated because of his asthma, which King likens to being frightened to death. King took notes on the police interrogation at the time and fictionalized the murder as part of the 1985 sequence of events.

Other events from Bangor's history—the death of a child in the Standpipe, the gang shooting in the downtown area during the Depression, the loggers' massacre—make it into the novel as well. King expressed fears at the time that he would "become persona non grata in my own town following the publication of this book" for revealing some of its sordid past.[96] Though Derry shares some features with Bangor, the two cities are geographically distinct in King's universe. Characters in this book and others are aware of both places. This permits King to claim artistic license when fictionalizing incidents that the Bangor Chamber of Commerce would probably prefer remain forgotten.

Despite the fact that Pennywise comes back to Derry every generation to plunder the city of its children, the city thrives. The adults have turned a blind eye to the city's dark underbelly, allowing evil free reign by simply doing nothing. The seven Losers discover that evil can prevail, but good can conquer evil if they band together. On their own, they are vulnerable, both to the town's bullies and to Pennywise. When they present a united front, they can defeat both. Granted, they are not completely alone—a turtle acts as a counterforce to Pennywise. It claims to have created the universe but now prefers to hide in its shell and allow things to happen without interfering. King calls the turtle "a symbol of everything that is stable in the universe . . . sanity in a world where we don't know where we came from or where we are going."[97]

The book's most controversial scene takes place near the end of the events of 1958, when the six boys consummate a sexual relationship with the group's lone female member. King says, "Beverly becomes the symbolic conduit between adulthood and childhood for the boys in the Losers' Club. It is a role that women have played again and again in the lives of boys: the symbolic advent of manhood through the act of sex."[98]

At some point during the seven years between the inspiration for *It* and when he finished the book, King's addiction problems expanded to include drugs. In a recent interview he said that cocaine helped at first. "It seemed like a really good energizing drug. You try some and think: wow, why haven't I been taking this for years? So you take a bit more and write a novel, and decorate the house, and mow the lawn and then you are ready to start a new novel again. . . . I didn't feel that happiness was enough: that there had to be a way to improve on nature. . . . Basically, I was an addict. I would take anything. In the daytime I used to be pretty straight, not getting blotto until five in the afternoon. But by the end I was a round-the-clock drink-and-drug addict."[99] Revisions to *It* were done in an alcohol-and-drug-fueled daze at the end of King's long days on the set of *Maximum Overdrive*, which he wrote and directed.

For nearly two years after completing *It*, King wasn't able to finish anything except for a few short stories. "That's why, when Peter [Straub] and I made our way through *The Talisman*, and I began work on *The Tommyknockers* and *The Napkins* [i.e., *Eyes of the Dragon*], I was so knocked over to learn that there was indeed life after *It*."[100]

EVIDENCE OF IT'S SURVIVAL

Although Pennywise seems to have been vanquished at the end of *It*, there are indications in King's later books that the monster may have survived.

When Tommy Jacklin travels to Derry in *The Tommyknockers*, he has a vision that he writes off as a hallucination: "a clown grinning up at him from an open sewer manhole—a clown with shiny silver dollars for eyes and a clenched white glove filled with balloons."

In *Dreamcatcher*, when Mr. Gray takes Jonesy to Standpipe Hill in Derry to deliver his deadly infection into the water supply, the alien is incensed to find that the Standpipe no longer exists—it was destroyed in the great flood of 1985. A statue—placed there by the Losers' Club—commemorates those lost in the storm. "Spray-painted across it in jagged red letters, also perfectly visible in the truck's headlights, was this further message: PENNYWISE LIVES."

The emotional vampire Dandelo that Roland, Oy, and Susannah encounter at the edge of the white lands of Empathica in *The Dark Tower* dubs the robot that keeps his road cleared in the wintertime "Stutterin' Bill"— the childhood nickname given to one of the main characters in *It*, Bill Denborough. In his final moments, Dandelo turns into "something that was no longer human. It was the face of a psychotic clown." King has stated that Dandelo is not Pennywise, but they may be from the same species.

VIKING PENGUIN HARDCOVER EDITION OF IT.

ENCLOSED

COPYEDITED PAGES These manuscript pages from *It* detail the tragic death of Georgie Denborough, and they bear the copy editor's notes about layout and grammatical mistakes. The copy editor is also rightfully aware of the complications of the use of the word "it;" note the checkmarks on page 18, for example, verifying that the word should not be capitalized in those instances.

KING CLOWNS AROUND WITH A GERMAN EDITION OF IT (TRANSLATED ES), PUBLISHED BY HEYNE.

7 NUMBER ONE FAN

"I AM IN TROUBLE HERE. THIS WOMAN IS NOT RIGHT."

Over the course of a fourteen-month period during 1986 and 1987, King went on a publishing spree, releasing *The Eyes of the Dragon*, *The Drawing of the Three*, *The Tommyknockers,* and *Misery*. Following this, he said that he was going on an extended hiatus from writing, perhaps for as long as five years. It wasn't the first time King announced plans to retire, nor would it be the last. Time has always proven King's retirements from writing to be temporary in nature.

This was a particularly bleak period in King's life. He was at the height of his cocaine and alcohol abuse. When confronted by his family and friends about his problems during an

intervention, he tried—unsuccessfully—to manage his addictions without going cold turkey. He started attending twelve-step meetings but struggled. It would be another two years before he finally got sober.

Though critical response to *The Tommyknockers* (written "with my heart running at a hundred and thirty beats a minute and cotton swabs stuck up my nose to stem the coke-induced bleeding"[101]) was generally negative, *Misery* ("the title quite aptly described my state of mind"[102]) was a hit and garnered a more positive review from the *New York Times* than usual, where it was called subtle and intriguing.[103]

Misery was inspired in part by John Fowles's *The Collector* and the Evelyn Waugh short story "The Man Who Loved Dickens." After reading the latter, King wondered what would happen if Dickens himself were held captive. He reflected in an interview, "Halfway through . . . I realized I was trying to express some of my own deepest fear-feelings: the sense of being trapped, the sense of having come from someplace like Africa and knowing I would never be able to get home, and trying to figure out what it was I was doing, why I was doing it, and why people were responding to it."[104]

The novel came together in his mind as the result of a dream he had while flying to England aboard the Concorde during the early 1980s; he dreamed about "a woman who held a writer

above TYPESCRIPT TITLE GRAPHIC FOR KING'S 1987 NOVEL MISERY.

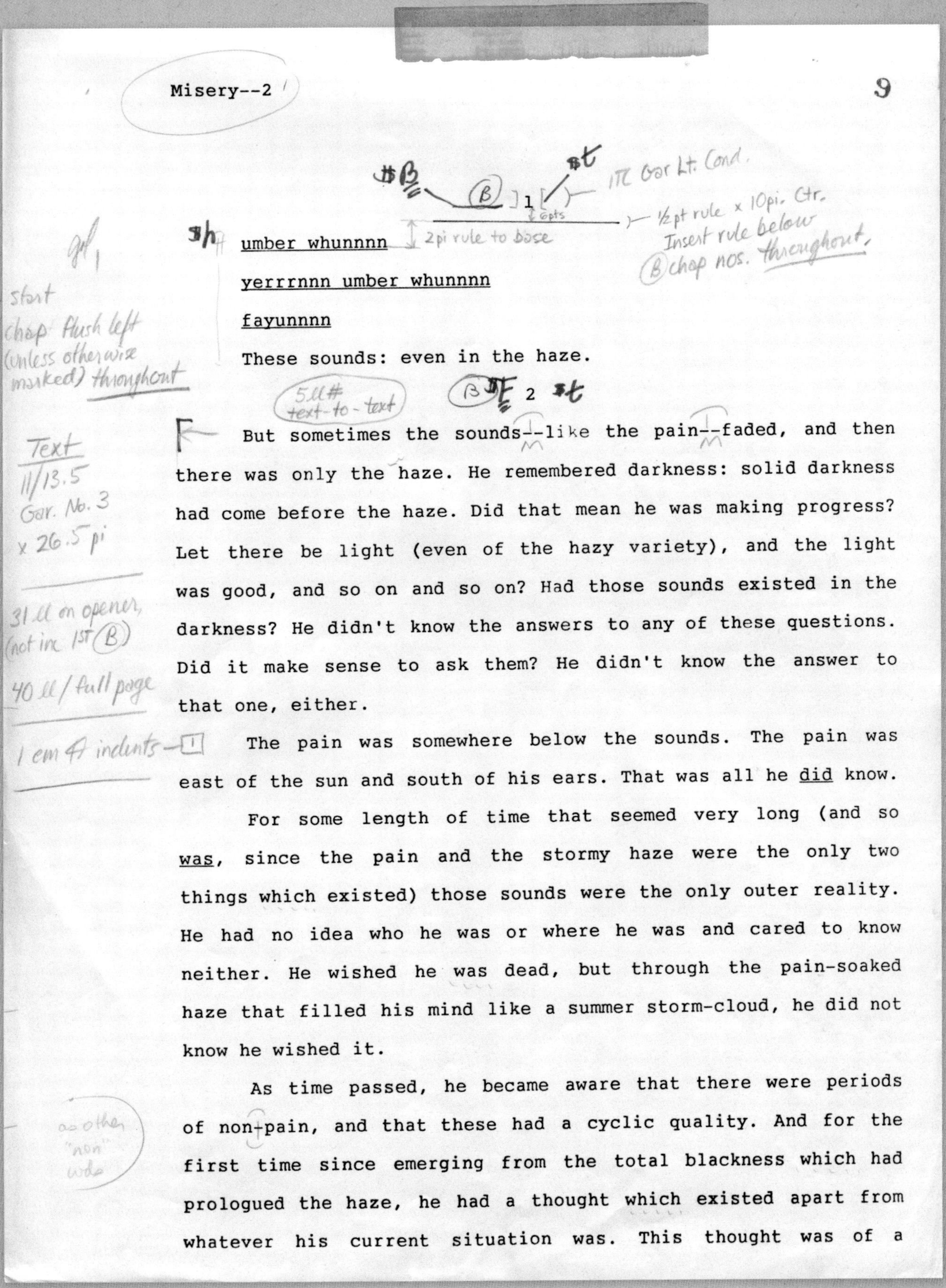

umber whunnnn

yerrrnnn umber whunnnn

fayunnnn

These sounds: even in the haze.

But sometimes the sounds--like the pain--faded, and then there was only the haze. He remembered darkness: solid darkness had come before the haze. Did that mean he was making progress? Let there be light (even of the hazy variety), and the light was good, and so on and so on? Had those sounds existed in the darkness? He didn't know the answers to any of these questions. Did it make sense to ask them? He didn't know the answer to that one, either.

The pain was somewhere below the sounds. The pain was east of the sun and south of his ears. That was all he did know.

For some length of time that seemed very long (and so was, since the pain and the stormy haze were the only two things which existed) those sounds were the only outer reality. He had no idea who he was or where he was and cared to know neither. He wished he was dead, but through the pain-soaked haze that filled his mind like a summer storm-cloud, he did not know he wished it.

As time passed, he became aware that there were periods of non-pain, and that these had a cyclic quality. And for the first time since emerging from the total blackness which had prologued the haze, he had a thought which existed apart from whatever his current situation was. This thought was of a

A COPYEDITED MANUSCRIPT PAGE FROM MISERY, CONTAINING ANNOTATIONS TO THE LAYOUT STAFF CONCERNING FONT SIZES, PARAGRAPH INDENTATION STYLES, AND SPACING BETWEEN LINES

King signs autographs for fans at a fundraiser for the
Charlotte Hobbs Memorial Library in Lovell, Maine, 2002.

prisoner and killed him, skinned him, fed the remains to her pig, and bound his novel in human skin."[105] When he woke up, he wrote this scene on a cocktail napkin so he wouldn't forget it: "She speaks earnestly but never quite makes eye contact. A big woman and solid all through; she is an absence of hiatus. 'I wasn't trying to be funny in a mean way when I named my pig Misery, no sir. Please don't think that. No, I named her in the spirit of fan love, which is the purest love there is. You should be flattered.'"[106]

King was unable to sleep after arriving in England, and the story continued to haunt him. He asked the concierge at Brown's Hotel in London if there was a quiet place where he could write. The man led him to a staircase landing where there was a desk that had once belonged to Rudyard Kipling.

That night, King filled sixteen pages of a steno notebook in longhand, ending where writer Paul Sheldon wakes up to find himself a prisoner of his number one fan, Annie Wilkes, one of the most colorful characters in all of King's fiction. King remembers, "When I called it quits, I stopped in the lobby to thank the concierge again for letting me use Mr. Kipling's beautiful desk. 'I'm so glad you enjoyed it,' he replied. He was wearing a misty, reminiscent little smile, as if he had known the writer himself. 'Kipling died there, actually. Of a stroke. While he was writing.' I went back upstairs to catch a few hours' sleep, thinking of how often we are given information we really could have done without."[107] Years later, while in England to promote *Lisey's Story*, King and his U.K. editor spent part of a day looking for the desk, but couldn't find it.

King thought he was working on a novella, which he planned to call *The Annie Wilkes Edition*. However, Paul Sheldon fought back from the fate King had conceived for him in his dream. "His efforts to play Scheherazade and save his life gave me a chance to say some things about the redemptive power of writing that I had long felt but never articulated," King said.[108]

Some readers interpreted *Misery* as an indictment of King's more ardent fans, especially because of the book's cryptic

FAN OR FANATIC?

Though Annie Wilkes may have been a metaphor for King's drug problems, he has had a couple of his own overzealous fans:

"*Misery* wasn't based on any kind of an atrocity. . . . I didn't have too many of the real fanatics at that time. But I've picked up one or two since. There was a guy who broke into my house who claimed he had a bomb and would explode it if I didn't listen to his ideas. I wasn't there. My wife came down at six o'clock in the morning, and this guy holds out a backpack and says, 'There's a bomb in here. I have to talk to Stephen King.' She ran out of the house in her nightgown to call the police. They came and arrested him. The bomb turned out to be pencils and erasers, and paperclips that had been pulled apart into wires. In his mind, this was a bomb."[109]

dedication. "This is for Stephanie and Jim Leonard, who know why. Boy, do they." Stephanie Leonard was King's personal assistant at the time and editor of *Castle Rock*, a monthly newsletter distributed from King's office to over 5,000 subscribers during the mid-to-late 1980s as a response to the flood of fan mail he was receiving. King agreed to the newsletter as a way of answering their most frequently asked questions and even contributed works of fiction and nonfiction occasionally, so long as he wasn't directly involved with it. The publication was a family affair—Stephanie Leonard is also King's sister-in-law. His mother-in-law handled the subscriptions.

Though King sees *Misery* as a love letter to his fans, the fans weren't so sure. Tabitha King responded to their letters

KING AT HIS DESK IN HIS HOME OFFICE, CIRCA 1980.

ENCLOSED

NEWSLETTER The inaugural issue of *Castle Rock*, a newsletter published by King's office staff as a way of coping with all of the fan mail he received. Starting with issue 5, the newsletter switched to a tabloid format that allowed for more elaborate layout and the inclusion of photographs. The newsletter ran until the end of 1989, with Stephanie Leonard editing for several years until she turned the reins over to Jim Leonard.

with an essay in *Castle Rock* that said in part, "I have read several pained, angry, and offended letters from fans who mistakenly believe that Steve was recording his true feelings about his readers in *Misery*. I take their distress as genuine and want to ease it if I can. If [Annie Wilkes] personifies any fan, it is perhaps Mark Chapman. Celebrity attracts madness as well as whole people. . . . Perhaps more importantly, Annie Wilkes is a metaphor for the creative drive itself. . . . *Misery* is concerned with the way in which a creative person can be tortured by his own powers, addicted to the act of creation, damaged by it."[110]

King's overzealous fan, Annie Wilkes, is given unique access to the object of her obsession, Paul Sheldon, the author of Victorian romance novels featuring heroine Misery Chastain. Annie is a former nurse once charged with killing patients in her neonatal ward. She was acquitted, but she was guilty of those and numerous other killings during her career.

Paul drops into her lap like manna from heaven when he veers off the road during a snowstorm while driving under the influence of too much champagne. He has just celebrated the completion of his first mainstream novel. For years he has felt pigeonholed as a romance writer, and he believes that *Fast Cars* might win both critical acclaim and prestigious literary awards. The only copy of the manuscript in existence, the result of two years' work, is with him when he crashes.

Annie stumbles upon the scene and rescues him from the wreckage. Both of Paul's legs are broken and he is unconscious. Instead of taking him to the hospital, she brings him to her isolated house, where she intends to nurse her idol back to health. Paul awakens to find himself immobilized in bed. The prescription painkillers Annie feeds him dull his senses.

above JAMES CAAN AS PAUL SHELDON IN THE CASTLE ROCK ENTERTAINMENT ADAPTATION OF <u>MISERY</u>, DIRECTED BY ROB REINER.

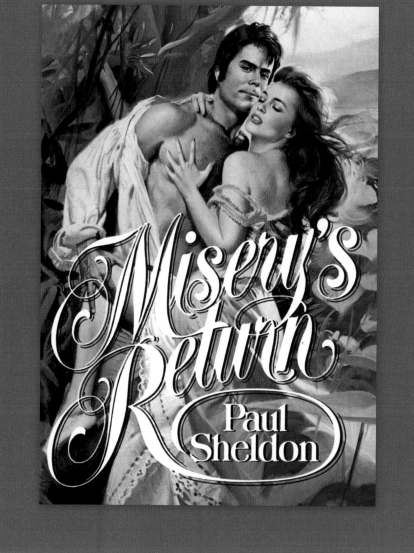

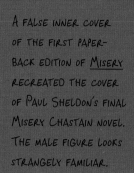

She discovers and reads *Fast Cars*. She doesn't like it, especially all the swearing. Annie has a strange relationship with cursing—she has invented an entire language of alternate words she uses to vent her frustrations and her rage. She forces Paul to burn the manuscript—a ritual of cleansing. Paul is still in incredible pain from the accident, and she threatens to withhold his medication to coerce him into complying.

Annie's economic circumstances prevent her from buying Paul's books in hardcover, so she doesn't know yet that Paul killed off the heroine in the latest book, *Misery's Child*. Once she finds out, she is enraged—but she also has a solution at her disposal. She has the creator under her complete control. She acquires all the things Paul needs to set up an office and tells him to write a novel that resurrects Misery

from the dead. The metaphor of a writer trapped in a genre is made real.

King plays with the classic tale of *One Thousand and One Nights*, in which Scheherazade forestalls her execution by telling the king an exciting story and promising an even better one the following night. The only way Paul can prolong his life and perhaps find a way to escape is to tell Annie the story she wants to hear, the next Misery Chastain novel. Properly motivated, he pours his heart and soul into the book and is surprised to discover that it's the best one he's ever written.

The first edition paperback of *Misery* contained an illustration depicting the cover of Paul's book *Misery's Return*, featuring a bare-chested Stephen King in a clinch with a raven-haired beauty.

right VIKING PENGUIN HARDCOVER EDITION OF MISERY.

THE MARK CHAPMAN STORY

For years, King believed that Mark David Chapman had approached him in Manhattan in the late 1970s after he filmed a segment of the *Today* show. This was the man who would, in 1980, murder John Lennon near Central Park.

The man not only asked for an autograph, he had his picture taken with King using a Polaroid camera and had King autograph the photograph as well. It's a good story, but, as it turns out, untrue. King may have signed an autograph for someone named Mark Chapman, but it wasn't Mark David Chapman, who was living in Hawaii at the time of the encounter outside Rockefeller Center. A *Washington Post* reporter investigating the story wrote that Chapman's limited finances made it unlikely he could have traveled to New York.

Another disturbed man has made a cottage industry out of trying to promote the idea that it was actually King and not Chapman who assassinated Lennon as part of a convoluted plot involving Ronald Reagan and Richard Nixon.

One of the amusing details in the book is the old Royal typewriter Annie buys for Paul that is missing the letter N, like the one King used as a child to write his first stories. Like King, Paul enters the missing letters by hand, an effect that is recreated in the extracts of Paul's manuscript that are reproduced in King's novel.

After Annie amputates Paul's foot with an axe following one of his escape attempts and cauterizes the stump with a propane torch, there's no longer any question about her sanity. At first, King thought that Annie should have a good side, because everyone does—or so he believed. But he says that, ultimately, "this voice rose up inside me and said, 'Why does she have to have a good side? If she's crazy, go ahead, make her a monster! She's a human being but let her be a monster if that's what she wants to be,' and it was such a relief!"[111]

In later years, King compared Annie Wilkes to Randall Flagg, someone who is "utterly and completely gonzo. Willing to do anything, not only to her 'pet writer' or any 'dirty bird' who happens to get in her way, but to herself.[112] However, he has a soft spot for her: "In the end, I felt that Annie was almost as much to be pitied as to be feared."[113]

King claims that *Misery* is about "how writers can live, and people with imaginations can live, even in miserable physical circumstances. People like that use their imagination as a cave where they can have a refuge."[114] The unspoken subtext of the novel, though, is King's real-life struggle with addiction. In later years, he has spoken openly about Annie as a metaphor for cocaine, with himself as the drug's pet writer: "There was never any question. Annie was my drug problem, and she was my number one fan. God, she never wanted to leave."[115]

In a brilliant stroke of irony, the weapon Paul ultimately uses against Annie is the Royal typewriter she bought him, the one with the missing letters that remind Paul of missing teeth and, later, of his missing foot. After he hits her with the typewriter, he stuffs pages from the *Misery's Return* manuscript into Annie's mouth. The writer defeats the monster with the tools of his trade and the product of his imagination.

In a real-life twist that might have come from one of his books, a woman sued King over *Misery*, claiming that Annie Wilkes was based on her. She also believed that King tapped her phone, hired helicopters to spy on her, burglarized her home, and stole manuscripts, which he later published under his name.

right THE PHOTOGRAPHER, ANDREW UNANGST, WHO ALSO TOOK KING'S AUTHOR PHOTO FOR THE HARDCOVER EDITION OF MISERY, SHOT THIS IMAGE FOR AN INTERVIEW MAGAZINE PIECE.

MOVIE STAR

In 1985, King agreed to film a commercial that featured him wearing a smoking jacket and carrying a candle as he walks through a haunted house. "Do you know me?" he intoned. "It's frightening how many novels of suspense I've written. But still, when I'm not recognized, it just kills me. So instead of saying I wrote *Carrie*, I carry the American Express card. Without it, life's a little scary."

That wasn't his first time in front of the camera. His big-screen debut was in a George Romero movie, *Knight Riders*, starring Ed Harris—who would later appear in the adaptation of *Needful Things* and *The Stand*. King and his wife play a couple of hecklers in the crowd—he is billed as the Hoagie Man because he's cramming a sandwich into his mouth at the time.

He played the title character in "The Lonesome Death of Jordy Verrill," one of the five segments in *Creepshow*, a movie that also featured a very young Joe King as the boy whose father throws away his horror comic books. (He gets his revenge with a voodoo doll at the end.)

King's other film and television appearances, over a dozen in total, have been cameo roles in adaptations of his novels and short stories, usually playing humorous characters. An ATM curses at him in *Maximum Overdrive*. He plays orchestra director Gage Creed (the same name as the young boy in *Pet Sematary*) in the miniseries version of *The Shining*, a pharmacist named Dr. Banghor in *Thinner*, and a pizza deliveryman in *Rose Red*.

KING AS JORDY VERRILL IN "THE LONESOME DEATH OF JORDY VERRILL"
SEGMENT OF <u>CREEPSHOW</u>, DIRECTED BY GEORGE A. ROMERO.

LAUREL SHOW, INC.   "CREEPSHOW"   Day/Date __Tuesday, 10/27/81__
(412) 325-2131   Day of Shooting _74_
                                        Crew Call   __8:00A__
Producer: RICHARD RUBINSTEIN   CALL SHEET   Camera Roll   __10:00A__
Director: GEORGE ROMERO   Coffee etc. _7:30A_ for 65
First AD: JOHN HARRISON   First Meal _2:00P_ for 65

      "We've got to keep a close watch on these damned bugs. They've never seen a
      white woman before." -Goose

D/N - INT/EXT - SCENE - DESCRIPTION	SCENE NOS.	LOCATION
D/INT. METEOROLOGISTS OFFICE	358 -368,	LAUREL STUDIOS
Jordy discusses the meteor with	396 - 399	
meteorologist.	(page 9 of shot list)	
N/INT. LIVING ROOM - TV - STAGE III	516	
Reindeer Shot.		
D/INT. BANK LOAN OFFICE	379-385	
Jordy discusses his loan with	(Page 10 of shot list)	
loan officer.		

CAST	CHARACTER	REPORT	MAKE-UP	ON-SET
STEPHEN KING	JORDY	9:00A	9:00A	9:30A
BINGO O'MALLEY	METEOROLOGIST	8:45A	8:45A	9:30A
	BANK LOAN OFFICER			

SPECIAL EFFECTS	PROPS
	METEOR
NONE TODAY	BROKEN METEOR
	BUCKET
THURSDAY - 10/29/81	WAD OF BILLS
FINAL STAGE	
JORDY'S SUICIDE	

CREW CALL				TRANSPORTATION	
Director	8:00A	Make-up	8:00A	DOWNTOWN:	7:00A
ADs	7:30A	Wardrobe	8:00A		
Script	8:00A	Props	8:00A	WQED:	7:20A
Camera	8:00A	SFX	Per Tom		
Asst Cam	8:00A	Loc Mgr	7:30A	ALCOMA:	7:45A
Sound	8:00A	Tran Mgr	Own Call		
Grips	8ish	Drivers	Per Levy		
Electric	8:00A	PAs	7:30A		
Scenic	8:00A	Stills	9:30A		

ADVANCE SCHEDULE	RAIN COVER
WEDNESDAY 10/28/81	None
N/INT. BATHROOM - 520-548 - Jordy speaks	
(Shot List Pg. 9) to his dad & takes a bath.	
D/INT. DOCTOR'S OFFICE 443-452 - Jordy discusses	
(Shot List Pg. 10) his fingers with the	
doctor.	

CALL SHEET FROM THE FILMING OF CREEPSHOW, WHICH SPECIFIES
THE TIME KING WAS SCHEDULED TO REPORT TO THE SET.

THE NIGHT JOURNEY

"SOMETIMES THERE IS ABSOLUTELY NO DIFFERENCE AT ALL BETWEEN SALVATION AND DAMNATION."

THE GREEN MILE

During the early 1980s, King self-published three installments of a book called *The Plant* using his personal press, Philtrum. This was King's first experiment with serial publication, though it didn't gain much attention at the time because the chapbooks were distributed privately.

A decade later he started working on a story called "What Tricks Your Eye," about a huge black man on death row "who develops an interest in sleight-of-hand as the date for his execution draws near. The story was to be told in the first person, by an old trusty who wheeled a cart of books through the cell blocks. . . . At the end of the story, just before his execution, I wanted the huge prisoner, Luke Coffey, to make himself disappear."[116]

King worked on the story in his mind while struggling with insomnia. Each night he would add a little bit more before finally falling asleep. Usually he got tired of these "cure for insomnia" stories and started a new one after a while.

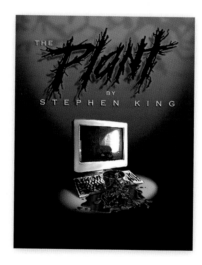

"What Tricks Your Eye" stuck with him longer than most, but he couldn't get it to work until a year and a half later, when he came up with a different slant: "Suppose . . . the big guy was a healer of some sort instead of an aspiring magician, a simpleton condemned for murders that he not only did not commit but had tried to reverse?"[117]

As promising as the idea seemed, King was too busy to write it. He remembers, "I had filled a notebook with scribbled pages . . . and realized I was building a novel when I should have been spending my time clearing my desk for revisions on [*Desperation*]."[118] He was also simultaneously working on the script for the miniseries version of *The Shining*.

While he was trying to decide whether to go on with or abandon the story, King's foreign rights agent, Ralph Vicinanza, showed his copies of *The Plant* to British editor Malcolm Edwards. During a conversation about the way books used to be published and how formulaic the business had become, Edwards wondered aloud whether it would be possible to

above COVER FOR THE ELECTRONIC EDITION OF KING'S ABORTED NOVEL THE PLANT. right KING AT A SIGNING IN FEBRUARY 1982, THE YEAR WHEN THE FIRST INSTALLMENT OF THE PLANT WAS PUBLISHED.

PHILTRUM PRESS

Philtrum Press is a private press owned and operated by Stephen King.

The first work to be published under the imprint was *The Plant*, issued as chapbooks in 1982, 1983, and 1985 and distributed in lieu of Christmas cards. Only two hundred numbered and twenty-six lettered copies were produced, along with an unknown number of designer's proofs.

A hallmark of Philtrum Press publications is the high-quality imported paper and understated design, the work of Michael Alpert, a classmate of King's at the University of Maine.

Other Philtrum publications include "The New Lieutenant's Rap," a modified excerpt from *Hearts in Atlantis* issued in conjunction with the twenty-fifth anniversary of the publication of *Carrie*; the collection *Six Stories*; the e-book *Riding the Bullet* (co-published with Simon & Schuster); later installments of *The Plant* distributed through King's Web site; and *The Ideal, Genuine Man* by Don Robertson, Philtrum's only non-King work.

The word *philtrum* refers to the vertical groove between a person's nose and his upper lip.

PARTS I, II, AND III OF <u>THE PLANT</u> HOUSED IN A CUSTOM TRAY-CASE FROM BETTS BOOKSTORE IN BANGOR.

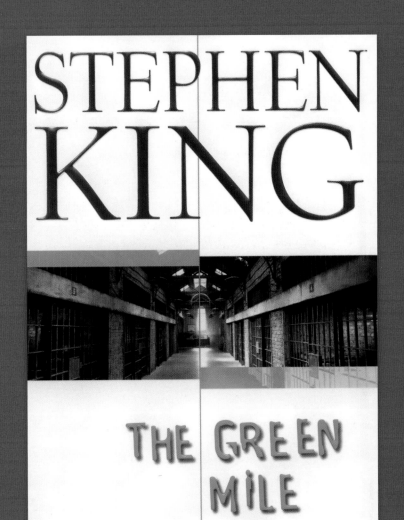

SCRIBNER'S HARDCOVER EDITION, RELEASED FOUR YEARS AFTER THE GREEN MILE FIRST APPEARED IN MONTHLY INSTALLMENTS.

produce a book in cheap installments, the way Charles Dickens's work had been published in the nineteenth century. The two men agreed that King was probably the only living author on whom publishers would risk releasing a book in sections while he was still writing it.

Vicinanza presented the idea to King, uncertain whether or not his client would be interested. King was. For one thing, it would give him the excuse he needed to set aside time to write his death-row novel, *The Green Mile*.

The book and its unique delivery system were both a critical and a publishing success. The fact that each installment went on sale on the same day across the continent—and also in translation in a number of other countries worldwide—meant that everyone was experiencing the story at the same rate. No one could "read ahead" and spoil the ending—for him- or herself or for anyone else. Online message boards were alive with discussion about the story and its intriguing characters, speculating about what would happen next month.

King's publisher fanned interest by taking advantage of the burgeoning Internet. Their Web site offered contests where readers could win prizes. They created a serial screensaver for computers that grew and expanded along with the book. TV advertisements were also made available on the Web site. From March through August 1996, *The Green Mile* was the focus of attention of King fans and the publishing industry alike.

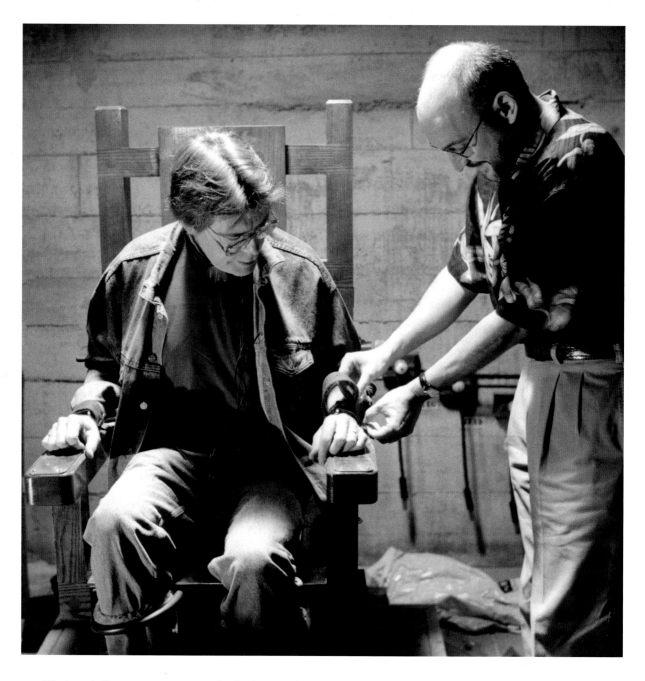

What made the process even more fascinating was the fact that King had not yet written the last installment when the first one appeared. He reveled in the danger of the approach, saying, "I liked the high-wire aspect of it, too: fall down on the job, fail to carry through, and all at once about a million readers are howling for your blood."[119] In a conversation with director Frank Darabont, while he was in the middle of Part III with only the vaguest idea of where the story was going, King said he was "probably getting ready to make the biggest mistake of my life."[120]

King said he "wrote like a madman" to keep up with the publishing schedule. His work was complicated by the requirement that each installment be the same length and end with a miniclimax. He also didn't have the luxury of backing up to change details if the story went in a different direction. He said that there was "less margin for screwing up—it had to be right the first time."[121] In the introduction to the first installment, King wrote, "It has certainly energized the writing of the story, although at this moment (a rainy evening in October of 1995) it is still far from done, even in rough draft, and the outcome

above DIRECTOR FRANK DARABONT STRAPS KING INTO THE ELECTRIC CHAIR ON THE SET OF THE GREEN MILE. right AN IMAGE FROM THE FILM ADAPTATION OF THE GREEN MILE: THE BAD DEATH OF EDUARD DELACROIX.

Brutus "Brutal" Howell (David Morse) and John Coffey (Michael Clark Duncan)
take one last walk down the Green Mile in the film.

remains in some doubt. That is part of the excitement of the whole thing, though—at this point I'm driving through thick fog with the pedal all the way to the metal."[122]

The book's release was a logistical nightmare. For six consecutive months, the publisher had to orchestrate the delivery and release of each installment on a specific date, which is a rare occurrence in paperback publishing. Booksellers were asked to sign documents binding them to the agreed-upon release dates for the books, to prevent them from going on sale early. The publisher's worst nightmare was that eager sellers would buy far too many copies of the first installment. Because of the way paperback returns are handled, the numbers wouldn't filter back to the publisher in time to make adjustments to the print runs for subsequent installments.

They needn't have worried. Part I, *The Two Dead Girls*, went straight to the top of the best-seller list, as did each subsequent installment of the serial. Eighteen million copies of the chapbooks ended up in print and King set a world record for having the most books on the best-seller list simultaneously in September 1996, when all six installments were on the *New York Times* list—a phenomenon that instigated a change in the way future serialized books were classified on the list.

The Green Mile takes place on E Block in Cold Mountain State Penitentiary in 1932 in an unspecified Southern state. As a framing device, King establishes a first-person narrator, Paul Edgecombe, the former block supervisor, who is recounting those long ago events from a Georgia nursing home.

E Block is the place where prisoners await their date with the electric chair. King says, "'Old Sparky' has fascinated me ever since my first James Cagney movie, and the first Death Row tales I ever read (in a book called *Twenty Thousand Years in Sing Sing*, written by Warden Lewis E. Lawes) fired the darker side of my imagination. What, I wondered, would it be like to walk those last forty yards to the electric chair, knowing you were going to die there? What, for that matter, would it be like to be the man who had to strap the condemned in . . . or pull the switch? What would such a job take out of you? Even creepier, what might it add?"[123]

The lives of the guardians of E Block are complicated by the introduction of a gentle giant, a simple man accused of the brutal murders of two young girls. He was found with the dead girls in his lap, and his statement upon arrest seemed to acknowledge his culpability. The character King first called Luke Coffey became John Coffey, and his touch could heal. "I decided to give him the initials J.C., after the most famous innocent man of all time," King said. "I wasn't sure, right up to the end of the book, if my J.C. would live or die. I wanted him to live because I liked and pitied him, but I figured those initials couldn't hurt, one way or the other."[124]

King also gives readers ample reason to question whether Coffey is guilty, and whether the electric chair is a fitting punishment for any person. Through the grotesquely botched execution of Eduard Delacroix (a symbolic name meaning "of the cross"), an endearing character who freely admits his guilt and is remorseful about his actions, King depicts the potential barbarism of capital punishment. Understandably, some readers drew conclusions about King's personal beliefs about it, but he counters, "I think there's an assumption, based on the book, that I'm against the death penalty. I'm not. I'm against it in ninety-nine percent of the cases where it's used. I believe it should be an absolute last resort. That it should never be used without eyewitness testimony that the crimes took place. There is only one justification for the death penalty that I understand: the people who are executed never do it again."[125]

> "WHAT, I WONDERED, WOULD IT BE LIKE TO WALK THOSE LAST FORTY YARDS TO THE ELECTRIC CHAIR, KNOWING YOU WERE GOING TO DIE THERE?"

The book's villains aren't the convicted killers on death row—except, perhaps, for William "Billy the Kid" Wharton, who is truly heinous. The villain in the piece is a system that treats everyone subject to it the same way and has no mechanism for compassion. Percy Wetmore is the embodiment of this system, a cruel, ambitious guard who has influential connections that guarantee his position on E Block. In the contemporary story, Wetmore seems to live on in the form of Brad Dolan, a nursing home orderly who makes the most of the little power afforded him by his position.

Though *The Green Mile* is ultimately a tragedy, a sense of optimism pervades it. John Coffey's heroism and compassion touch everyone he encounters during his stay on E Block—and especially during one unauthorized night journey to the warden's house to cure his wife's cancer. Seventy years later, Paul Edgecombe is a living testament to Coffey's lasting gift, although it is an open question whether Paul's longevity is a boon or a curse.

The Green Mile wasn't King's only publishing experiment in 1996. One month after the final installment hit bookshelves, two more novels were published on the same day. One of them, *Desperation*, was attributed to Stephen King, the other, *The Regulators*, was attributed to Richard Bachman, a pseudonym King hadn't used since *Thinner* in 1984. The two novels were different in setting, tone, and plot, but shared the same cast of characters, although the relationships among the characters were upended from one book to the other. King likened the experiment to a repertory theater troupe acting in two different plays on subsequent nights. It was a big year for his publisher, with the promise of a new installment in King's Dark Tower series in the coming months. However, it was to be King's last year with Viking Penguin. After nearly two decades, he decided it was time for a fresh start.

right STEPHEN KING, CIRCA 1996.

DOLLAR BABIES

The Shawshank Redemption wasn't the first adaptation of a King work by Frank Darabont, who also directed *The Green Mile* and *The Mist*. In the 1980s, Darabont acquired, for the princely amount of $1, noncommercial rights to adapt King's short story "The Woman in the Room," one of the first of a series of projects that became known as "dollar babies."

King's accountant wasn't very happy with the idea, because it was fraught with potential legal problems, but King continues to grant one-time rights to student filmmakers to make a movie out of any short story where the film rights are still available. He has a few conditions: "I ask them to sign a paper promising that no resulting film will be exhibited commercially without approval, and that they send me a videotape of the finished work."[126]

The movies can only be exhibited at film festivals or in other venues where admission is free. They cannot be made available for viewing or download over the Internet (with one exception, an eight-minute adaptation of the poem "Paranoid: A Chant") nor can they be distributed on DVD.

A few of King's short stories have been filmed numerous times by different directors. However, once King sells commercial movie rights to a story, the story is no longer available under this program.

The films vary widely in quality, style, and approach. Some are animated, though most are live action. A few have been adapted in foreign languages. King typically has no involvement with these productions, although he did contribute a voice cameo to an adaptation of "Lunch at the Gotham Café."

ENDRE HULES AND CULLEN DOUGLAS AS GUY, THE CRAZED MAITRE D', IN THE SHORT FILM "STEPHEN KING'S GOTHAM CAFÉ."

PARANOID/A Chant

I can't go out no more.
There's a man by the door
in a raincoat

smoking a cigarette.
But
I've put him in my diary
and the mailers are all lined up
on the bed, bloody in the glow
of the bar sign next door.

He knows that if I die
or even drop out of sight
the diary goes and everyone knows
the CIA's in Virginia.

500 mailers bought from
500 different drugcounters
and stationers shops and fifty pages
in each one.

I can see him from up here.
The city's alive with a million eyes.

His cigarette winks from just
above his trenchcoat collar
and somewhere there's a man on a subway
sitting under the ads and thinking my name.
Men have discussed me in back rooms.
If the phone rings, there's only dead breath.

In the bar across the street a snubnose
revolver has changed hands in the men's room
and each bullet has my name on it.
My name is written in back files
and looked up in the morgues of news offices.

My mother has been investigated;
thank God she's dead.

They have writing samples
and examine the back loops of pees
and the cross of tees;

my brother's with them.
His wife is Russian and he
keeps asking me to fill out forms. I
have it in my diary. Listen:

In the rain, at the bus stop,
black crows with black umbrellas
pretend to look at their watches, but
it's not raining. Their eyes are silver dollars.
Some are scholars in the pay of the FBI
which supports the foreigners who pour
through our streets. I fooled them
and got off the bus at 25th and 8th
where a cabby watched me over his newspaper.

THE ORIGINAL MANUSCRIPT OF "PARANOID: A
CHANT," A POEM FIRST PUBLISHED IN KING'S
COLLECTION SKELETON CREW. THE POEM WAS
ADAPTED INTO AN EIGHT-MINUTE SHORT FILM
BY JAY HOLBEN IN 2000.

PARANOID/2

In the room above me an old woman
has put an electric suption cup on her
floor. It sends rays through my light fixture
and now I write in the dark
by the bar-sign's glow.
I know.

They sent me a dog with brown spots
and a radio cobweb in its nose.
I drowned it in the sink and wrote it up
and put it in folder GAMMA.

I don't look in the mailbox anymore.
They want to letter-bomb me with greeting cards.

The luncheonette is laid with talking floors
and the waitress says it was salt she put
on my hamburger but I know arsenic when I
see it. And the hot yellow taste of mustard
to mask the bitter odor of almonds.

I have seen strange lights in the sky
and seen their cruising eyes.
Last night a dark man crawled through 9 miles
of sewer to surface in my toilet, listening
for phone calls through the cheap wood with
chrome ears. I xxix hsaw his muddy handprints
on the porcelain.

I don't answer the phone now.
Have I told you that?

They are planning to flood the earth with sludge.
They are planning breakins.
They are planning weird sex positions.
They are making addictive laxatives
and suppositories that burn the anal channel.
Their scientists know how to put out the sun
with blowguns.

I pack myself in ice, have I told you that?
It lowers body-heat and obviates their infrascopes.
I know many chants. I wear many charms.
You think you have me but I could destroy you
any second now.

Any second now.

Any second at all.

Did I tell you I can't go out no more?
There's a man by the door
in a raincoat.

9 THINGS THAT GO BUMP

"I'VE PUT DOWN MY SCRIVENER'S PEN. THESE DAYS I PREFER NOT TO."

BAG OF BONES

In October 1994, King rode his motorcycle across the United States, appearing at ten independent bookstores from Vermont to California in support of his novel *Insomnia*. Three years later, shortly after the miniseries version of *The Shining* aired on television, King decided to take a rare overseas vacation, this time riding his motorcycle across the Australian plains, ending with a public reading of "Autopsy Room Four" in Sydney, his only public appearance during the trip.

While he was away, a firestorm swept through the publishing world. News emerged that King had reached an impasse in contract negotiations with his current publisher, which had been subject to a series of corporate mergers, and that his next manuscript was up for bid. "I had gotten a bit stale at Viking, and we had reached a point where we were a bit too comfortable with each other,"[127] King says.

When superstar authors are involved in contract negotiations at this level, auctions are usually confidential. In this case, however, King's attorney sent queries to several publishers simultaneously and, when news leaked out, the process quickly made headlines. One publisher was quoted as saying that he thought the letter was a joke being played on him by a friend, but it was no joke. King's lawyer started meeting with interested parties.

Ultimately, an agreement was reached with Scribner to publish King's next three books. The deal was unusual. Instead of taking a massive advance, which had been the subject of many headlines, King entered into a risk-and-profit-sharing agreement. Advances for big-name authors like King had reached levels where the books were no longer profitable for the publisher. King's advance would be a relatively modest $2 million, but his share of royalties would be much greater. If a book did well, his publisher and he both benefited. If a book didn't meet expectations, the publisher wouldn't be on the hook for a major loss.

King later regretted that the search for a new publisher attracted so much publicity, saying, "I know we did it the wrong way . . . Hopefully, in the end, the talk will be about the book and not about the negotiations."[128] In another interview he said, "If I could do it all over again, I'd have asked Scribner for a dollar a book."[129]

King's first novel to be published under the Scribner imprint was *Bag of Bones*. To prepare for its marketing campaign, Scribner conducted focus groups to identify readers who had fallen away from King and those who knew of his works only

King during his 1997 motorcycle trip across Australia.

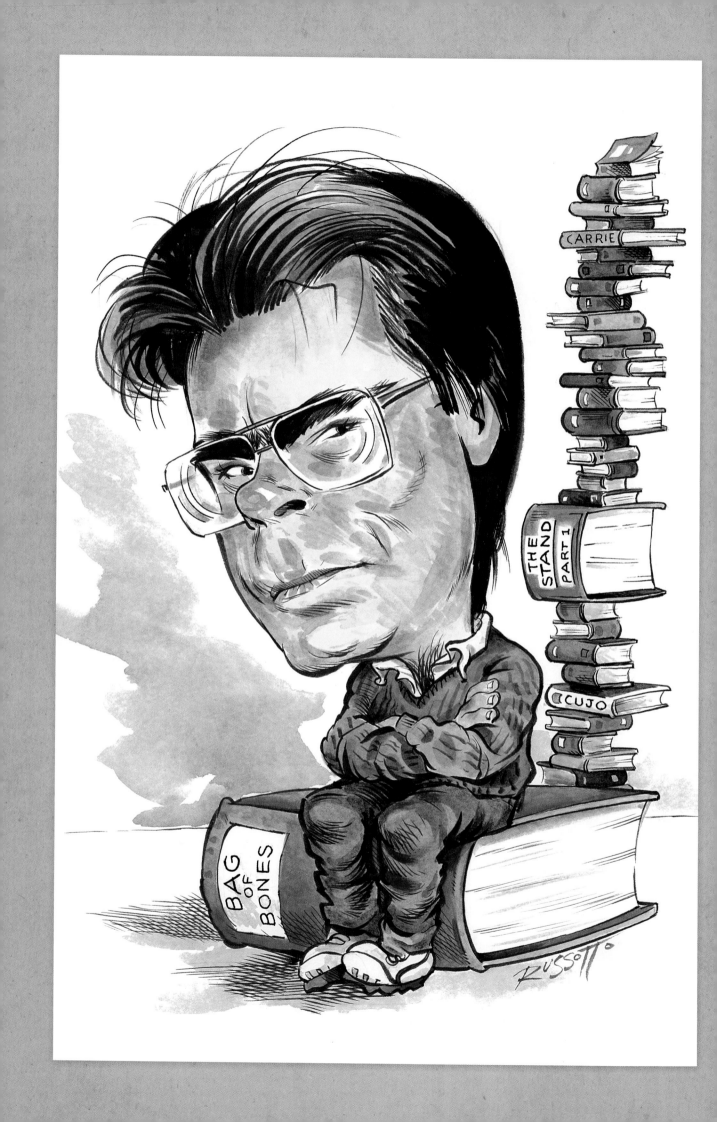

through film adaptations. They downplayed the horror aspect and played up the book's literary and romantic sides.

King's perspective was: "I wanted to write a gothic novel, and for me that is a novel about secrets. About things that happened in the past that have been buried and stay quiet for a while and then, like a buried body, they start to smell bad. If you believe in ghosts, in spooks, in things that go bump in the night, they start to move around a little bit and maybe they start to disturb your sleep a little bit. . . . I love the idea of secrets and secrets always find their way out."[130] In a promotional interview for the book, King said that *Bag of Bones* "contains everything I know about marriage, lust, and ghosts."

Bag of Bones is the story of mid-list novelist Mike Noonan, who has reached a plateau in his career. Early in the book, his wife, Jo, dies of a catastrophic stroke in the parking lot of a Derry pharmacy. Among the items in her shopping bag: a home pregnancy test. Mike and Jo have been trying to have a child for years, so the pregnancy test comes as a surprise to Mike. It makes him wonder what other secrets his late wife might have been keeping from him. King provides this insight into the ways his wife, Tabitha, his ideal reader, regularly contributes to his books: "In the first draft all [Jo] had in her purse was her ordinary rickrack and a piece of candy—the last thing that she'd bought on earth before dying. And Tabby said to me, 'She's pregnant. What if she had a home pregnancy test in there?' I said, 'That'd be fantastic!' So immediately I dumped it in there."[131]

One of the strange and lingering effects of his new status as a widower is that Mike acquires the world's worst case of writer's block. The simple act of opening up the word

---

left ARTIST RAY RUSSOTTO'S CARICATURE OF KING PERCHED ON HIS MOST RECENT NOVEL, BAG OF BONES.

as long as five years. As she sprinted across the parking lot toward the accident, that weak vessel in her cerebral cortex had blown like a tire, drowning her control-centers in blood and killing her. Death had probably not been instantaneous, the assistant medical examiner told me, but it had still come swiftly enough...and she wouldn't have suffered. Just one big black nova, all sensation and thought gone even before she hit the pavement.

The autopsy revealed something else, as well, something which I believe was then revealed to me by oversight...certainly there was no need for me to know, at least in their view. At the time of her death in the Rite Aid parking lot, Jo had been six weeks pregnant.

do this differently pregnancy test.

The days leading up to the funeral and the funeral itself are dreamlike in my memory--the clearest memory I have is of eating Jo's chocolate "sundry" and crying...crying mostly, I think, because I knew how soon the taste of it would be gone. I had one other crying fit a few days after we buried her, and I will tell you about that one shortly.

Does he find pregnancy test in purse or "prescription bag"?

FIRST DRAFT MANUSCRIPT PAGE FROM BAG OF BONES. KING'S WIFE SUGGESTED THAT HE ADD A PREGNANCY TEST TO THE ITEMS FOUND AMONG JO NOONAN'S PURCHASES ON THE DAY SHE DIED.

examiner told me, but it had still come swiftly enough...and she wouldn't have suffered. Just one big black nova, all sensation and thought gone even before she hit the pavement.

"Can I help you in any way, Mr. Noonan?" the assistant ME asked, turning me gently away from the still face and closed eyes on the video monitor. "Do you have questions? I'll answer them if I can."

"Just one," I said. I told him what she'd purchased in the drugstore just before she died. Then I asked my question.

The days leading up to the funeral and the funeral itself are dreamlike in my memory--the clearest memory I have is of eating Jo's chocolate mouse and crying...crying mostly, I think, because I knew how soon the taste of it would be gone. I had one other crying fit a few days after we buried her, and I will tell you about that one shortly.

I was glad for the arrival of Jo's family, and particularly for the arrival her oldest brother, Frank. It was Frank Arlen--fifty, red-cheeked, portly, and with a head of startlingly lush, almost

"THERE ARE PROBABLY A FEW CRITICS OUT THERE WHO WISH I HAD A LITTLE MORE WRITER'S BLOCK."

two books, so he has four manuscripts squirreled away in a safety deposit box. All he needs to do to keep the well-oiled machinery of his modest publishing career in motion is to make an annual withdrawal from the vault. King takes a gentle poke at the business by having Mike's editor compliment him on the newfound maturity in his work—that he is "taking it to the next level"—when she is actually discussing a manuscript he wrote nearly a dozen years earlier.

Readers wondered if King had manuscripts stockpiled, too, but that wasn't the case. He says, "There might have been a time in my life where I had two or three [books] stacked up. The inspiration for that detail in *Bag of Bones* came from a rumor I heard that Danielle Steel was writing three books a year and publishing two. And I was saying, If that's true over the last ten years, she must have a lot piled up."[133]

Mike stays in Derry for the next four years, spending most of his free time playing Scrabble and doing crossword puzzles on his computer. He becomes a metaphorical bag of bones, an expression that Mike derives from a statement he attributes to Thomas Hardy: "Compared to the dullest human being actually walking about on the face of the earth and casting his shadow there, the most brilliantly drawn character in a novel is but a bag of bones." The quote may not actually be from Hardy, but the allusion is appropriate, since Hardy stopped writing fiction after his novels—although very successful—received vocal public criticism.

At night, Mike dreams of Sara Laughs, the Noonans' summer home in western Maine, named by the local residents long before he and Jo acquired it after he retired from his job as a newspaper reporter to write full time. His dreams remind him of the opening line of Daphne du Maurier's novel *Rebecca*: "Last night I dreamt I went to Manderley again." Though he dreams of the house, it never occurs to Mike to go there.

When his final book from the vault really catches his publisher's interest and they want to open negotiations for a new multi-book contract worth millions of dollars, Mike decides to

processing program on his computer sends him into waves of nausea. He keeps his affliction secret from everyone—including his aggressive agent and his publisher. "Mike is probably as close as you could get to me," King says, "even though I've been careful to distance myself from him. He's not as successful, he has no children, his wife is dead, and he has writer's block. But our take on what writing is about and how the writing works is very similar."[132] Shortly after the book was released, King joked, "There are probably a few critics out there who wish I had a little more writer's block."

Mike can afford to hide his affliction. Although he has published a book a year for the past decade—the same time span as his marriage—during four of those years he wrote

CANDID PHOTOS OF KING AT WORK AND AT PLAY IN HIS OFFICE IN THE LATE 1990s.

THE ROCK BOTTOM REMAINDERS

King's affection for music is no secret. *Christine* is riddled with lyrics from classic songs, and it was King, not his publisher, who had to pay for the rights to reproduce them. He has played on stage with John Mellencamp and Jakob Dylan and makes an uncredited appearance on the track "It's Killing Me" on Michael McDermott's third album. "He knows some chords," McDermott said of King's guitar-playing abilities.[134]

When publicist Kathy Kamen Goldmark invited King to join a band composed of authors and music critics, along with a few "real" musicians, he didn't hesitate. The Rock Bottom Remainders (a "remainder" is a book that appears in a discount bin at a bookstore—it's not a flattering term) made their debut at a pair of charity concerts at the American Booksellers Association conference in Anaheim in 1992. Other band members at the time included Dave Barry, Ridley Pearson, Amy Tan, Roy Blount Jr., and Barbara Kingsolver.

The next year, the group went on tour, playing in six cities to raise money for teen literacy projects. A book of essays and photographs detailed their experiences: *Mid-life Confidential: The Rock Bottom Remainders Tour America with Three Chords and an Attitude.* Dave Barry likes to say that the group plays music as well as Metallica writes novels and describes their genre as "hard-listening" music.

Other writers have joined the group for their infrequent concerts over the years, including Carl Hiaasen, Mitch Albom, and Scott Turow, and they have been joined on stage by the likes of Warren Zevon, Roger McGuinn, and, on one memorable occasion, Bruce Springsteen.

TABITHA KING CAPTURED THIS PHOTO OF MUSICAL DIRECTOR AL KOOPER, COLUMNIST DAVE BARRY (BACKGROUND), AND STEPHEN KING PERFORMING AT A ROCK BOTTOM REMAINDERS CONCERT IN 1994.

get away. He can't explain his dilemma to anyone. Like Lisey Landon in *Lisey's Story*, the root of Mike's problem is that he's afraid of moving ahead with life without his spouse, that if he starts writing again, everything he had with Jo might unravel.

His dreams of Sara Laughs change subtly over time, as if the house is beckoning to him. At the same time, he feels like something dangerous is waiting for him there—an entity he associates with the ghost of Mrs. Danvers, the creepy housekeeper from *Rebecca*. Taking the advice of Ralph Roberts, the protagonist from *Insomnia*, Mike decides to go on vacation—and where better than at the house on Dark Score Lake?

King says, "What I really wanted to do was see if I could bring *Rebecca* into the next century. . . . Rebecca was not the person the narrator thinks she was. I thought, Turn that inside out. Suppose the narrator finds out that his wife was involved with a lot of things he didn't know about, and he comes back to this place suspecting she was there and discovers something else entirely."[135]

Shortly after Mike arrives in the unincorporated township called TR-90, several things happen that change his life. First, he believes that Sara Laughs is haunted—perhaps by the ghost of his late wife. He starts receiving messages, spelled out with refrigerator magnets, for example. He also senses a presence while exploring the house for clues about his wife's activities.

Interviewers often ask King if he has ever written anything that frightened him. Though he usually says no, he admits that part of *Bag of Bones* has had a lasting effect. He describes the scene in detail: "Mike Noonan goes downstairs to look for something in the cellar, and the door shuts behind him, and something begins to thump on the wall insulation. And he realizes that he's with a spirit he can talk to by asking 'yes' or 'no' questions, and the thing will thump once for 'yes' and twice for 'no.' And I found myself visualizing our stairway in our home, which has insulation on the walls. . . . So that now, whenever I go down the stairwell, I'm immediately reminded of that scene in the book, and I'm afraid that the door's going to swing shut

above KING CHATS WITH JAY LENO ON SEPTEMBER 24, 1998, FOUR DAYS AFTER BAG OF BONES WAS RELEASED.

She's also vulnerable. Mattie's husband was killed in a freak accident and her father-in-law, a malevolent Bill Gates character, is trying to get custody of her daughter, Kyra. Enough people witnessed the incident on the side of the road that it provides testimony against Mattie's mothering skills. Mike decides to help Mattie, using his considerable savings to fund her legal battle.

As he falls in love, he comes to life again. He even starts to write. At first he thinks that the secret to solving his block was getting away from his computer and working at an old electric IBM typewriter, but there's more going on than that. The boys in the basement, the muses who do the heavy work of inspiring his novels, have a message they're trying to convey on behalf of someone else, coded into his new manuscript. He starts to wonder if ghosts can be crazy—if a person's essence might survive, but without its sanity intact.

In addition to *Rebecca* and the works of Thomas Hardy and W. Somerset Maugham, one of the strongest literary influences on *Bag of Bones* is Herman Melville's short story "Bartleby the Scrivener," which Mattie Devore is reading as part of her book group. It's about a man who gradually retreats from life, repeatedly refusing requests with the phrase "I prefer not to."

Bag of Bones ends on a similar note. After unraveling a convoluted tale of a past crime that has been covered up for generations, Mike Noonan decides to quit writing. "I've lost my taste for spooks. . . . I've put down my scrivener's pen. These days I prefer not to." Many readers saw this as King's official notice of his intent to retire, or to at least change gears. King himself said, "As I began work on *Bag of Bones*, I looked a few sheets down the calendar and saw fifty staring me in the face. . . . Fifty is a dangerous age, a time when a writer may have to find a few new pitches if he's going to continue to be successful."[138]

In fact, it was something of a new beginning for King—the start of critical acceptance for his work. However, barely nine months after the book was published, an accident happened that permanently altered King's life.

behind me and the lights are going to go out and something's going to start thumping on the wall."[136]

Mike also acquires a love interest and a cause. While driving to lunch one day, he narrowly misses running over a little girl on the side of Route 68. A few minutes later he meets the girl's distraught mother—Mattie Devore, a single mother who he immediately dismisses as trailer trash. However, his first impression is quickly overturned and he finds himself attracted to someone barely half his age. "Here's a guy that's been grieving for four years," King explains. "It's been raining in his life for four years. And she's the first ray of sunshine that he sees. He's sexually attracted to her—she's young, she's beautiful, she's vivacious, she has all of that energy. What he sees in her is a kind of joyfulness."[137]

above KING READS FROM BAG OF BONES AT ROCKEFELLER PLAZA IN NEW YORK, SEPTEMBER 27, 1998.

THE PHILANTHROPIST

The Kings are well known in Maine for philanthropy, though their efforts often reach beyond the borders of their home state. Many school and town libraries have been the beneficiaries of grants, and several major development projects in Bangor have been funded in large part by the Kings, including the so-called "Field of Screams" baseball field (Mansfield Park), a swimming complex, hospital wings, and the Bangor Public Library.

The Stephen and Tabitha King Foundation is a private nonprofit organization that supports community initiatives. The Barking Foundation provides grants and scholarships for postsecondary education for Maine residents based on merit and financial need. These foundations are occasionally cited as being among the most efficient celebrity charitable organizations, with overheads typically on the order of a tenth of a percent.

After audio narrator Frank Muller was seriously injured in a motorcycle accident, King started the Wavedancer Foundation to provide support for people in the performing arts who are unable to work and have no health insurance. He arranged a public reading with John Grisham, Peter Straub, Pat Conroy, and himself to help fund the organization.

This organization morphed into the Haven Foundation, which was the recipient of the royalties from King's novel *Blaze* (released under the pseudonym Richard Bachman) and the proceeds from a two-night event at Radio City Music Hall that featured numerous famous emcees, with J. K. Rowling, John Irving, and King as readers.

KING HELPING A MIDDLE-SCHOOL STUDENT WITH A WRITING PROJECT.

10 THE ACCIDENT

"LIFE ISN'T A SUPPORT-SYSTEM FOR ART.
IT'S THE OTHER WAY AROUND." — STEPHEN KING

D uring a road trip from Florida to Maine in early 1999, King stopped at a gas station in Pennsylvania. While stretching his legs behind the station, he slipped, tumbled down a slope, and nearly ended up in a swollen stream at the bottom. The incident made him wonder how long it would have taken for someone to realize he was missing and to find him—or his body—in the gulley. Two months later, in the middle of June, he finished the first draft of *From a Buick 8*, a novel inspired by that incident.

Instead of conducting research beforehand, King prefers to complete a draft and then determine what is necessary. He says, "When I'm writing a book, my attitude is: don't confuse me with facts."[139] In this case, a return to Pennsylvania was in order, to visit with troopers and state police to learn the details of their daily lives. It would be fourteen months before King would get a chance to make that research junket.

That June, King and his wife were staying at their summer home on a lake in western Maine—a place very much like Sara Laughs from *Bag of Bones*. After completing *From a Buick 8*, he returned his attention to a nonfiction book he'd started a year and a half earlier called *On Writing*. At that

time, uncertain how or if to continue with the project after five or six months of work, he'd put it aside with only the "C.V." section completed.

On June 17, 1999, after rereading the manuscript fragment and discovering that he liked it, he made a list of the questions about writing he wanted to address in the book. The next day he wrote the first four pages of the "On Writing" section.

On June 19, he made the long, slow journey along Maine's country roads to Portland, where he delivered his son Owen to the airport. The rest of the family was planning to go to a movie in New Hampshire that evening, but King had time after he returned home for a nap and his traditional afternoon four-mile walk. His route: "Three miles of this walk are on dirt roads which wind through the woods; a mile of it is on Route 5, a two-lane blacktop highway which runs between Bethel and Fryeburg."[140]

As usual, King was reading during his walk—*The House* by Bentley Little. However, when he reached a short, steep hill with poor sight lines, he lowered the book so he could watch for oncoming traffic. He remembers what happened next clearly: "I was three-quarters of the way up this hill when Bryan Smith, the owner and operator of the Dodge van, came over the crest.

right COVER OF THE SCRIBNER EDITION OF FROM A BUICK 8. THE NOVEL OPENS WITH A PENNSYLVANIA STATE TROOPER BEING STRUCK BY A DRUNK DRIVER, AN EERILY PRESCIENT DEPICTION OF WHAT WOULD HAPPEN TO KING LESS THAN TWO MONTHS AFTER HE WROTE THE PASSAGE.

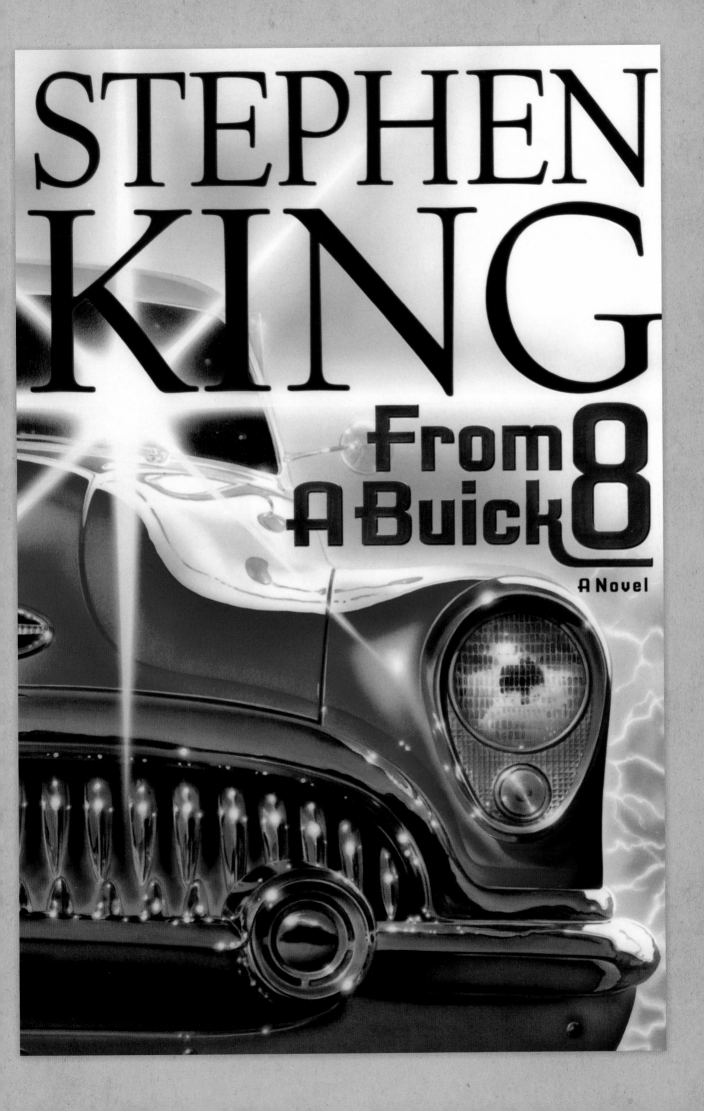

STEPHEN KING

From A Buick 8

A Novel

He wasn't on the road; he was on the shoulder. *My* shoulder. I had perhaps three-quarters of a second to register this."[141]

In the opening pages of *From a Buick 8*, State Trooper Curtis Wilcox is struck and killed by a drunk driver who is leaning over to extract a beer from a cooler on the floor next to him. When the book was published three years later, that incident seemed like it had been inspired by King's experience that June afternoon. However, it was a case of life imitating art, for King had written that scene months earlier.

Bryan Smith had a cooler in his van—it was behind him, though, and his Rottweiler Bullet was nosing at it to get at the raw meat inside. Smith ignored the road and turned to chastise the dog. The van drifted onto the shoulder, making a beeline for King, who turned slightly at the last minute—an instinctive move that probably saved his life.

One of the most chilling indications of the brutality of the impact is the fact that King's eyeglasses ended up on the front seat of Smith's van. Intimately familiar with stories that describe events as being like something out of his novels, King experienced something similar when Smith returned to see how badly injured he was. He later wrote, "It occurs to me that I have nearly been killed by a character right out of one of my own novels. It's almost funny."[142]

King's injuries were severe. While being transported to the hospital, his lung collapsed, necessitating a chest tube. One leg was so badly broken below the knee that a doctor described the bones as being like "marbles in a sock." His knee was split down the middle and his hip was fractured in two places. His spine was chipped in eight places and four ribs were broken. The flesh above his collarbone was stripped raw, and he required twenty or thirty stitches to close a laceration in his scalp.

After a week of complicated procedures to insert pins and rods into his leg, he was finally able to get out of bed for the first time. This was just the beginning of his ordeal, though. For someone with King's addiction history, dealing with

left HEADSHOT OF KING BY REX RYSTEDT, JANUARY 2002. above A CAR TRAVELS ON ROUTE 5 IN LOVELL, MAINE, PAST THE SITE WHERE KING WAS STRUCK BY DRIVER BRYAN SMITH ON JUNE 19, 1999.

KING'S FIRST PUBLIC APPEARANCE AFTER THE ACCIDENT WAS WITH HIS WIFE, TABITHA, AT THE PREMIERE OF THE GREEN MILE AT THE ZIEGFIELD THEATER IN NEW YORK, DECEMBER 8, 1999.

powerful pain medication was a challenge. He had been sober for over a decade. He recounts that "the doctor asked me where my pain was on a scale of one to ten and I said eleven, and he offered me a breakthrough, time-release pain killer called Oxycon. So I took the pills until I didn't need them anymore. I continued to take them because pain is subjective. But the addict part of my brain began inventing pain just to get these painkillers so I could have more of the drug. I had to kick it the way a junkie kicks heroin. It was a two-week process. I didn't sleep for two weeks. My feet twitched uncontrollably—that is why it is called kicking the habit, your feet literally kick out. It was horrible."[143]

Two weeks after the accident, he was able to sit up in a wheelchair for the first time. A week after that, he was allowed to return home, where he underwent a daily rehab program

to rebuild strength and mobility in his crushed leg. In August, he had surgery to remove the pins that protruded from his upper thigh.

News of King's accident spread quickly. While the response was generally sympathetic, his popularity made him an obvious target for the late-night talk-show hosts. They made jokes about how many books he had written while in the hospital, but to King, these jokes were not the least bit funny. He was truly worried that he might never be able to write again—that the chronic pain he would suffer for the rest of his life would destroy any creative impulses within him.

He had ample reason not to write. He was restricted to a walker and couldn't sit up for long periods of time. However, when he decided he wanted to go back to work, his wife

TIME

DO-IT-YOURSELF .COM

If Stephen King can do it, so can you. Who needs Hollywood when you can make your own movies, books and music?

TIME MAGAZINE'S MARCH 27, 2000, ISSUE FEATURED A COVER STORY ABOUT KING'S EXPERIMENT IN "ELIMINATING THE MIDDLE MAN" BY PUBLISHING HIS NOVELLA RIDING THE BULLET ON THE INTERNET.

MOVIE POSTER FOR MICK GARRIS'S 2004 ADAPTATION OF RIDING
THE BULLET, THE FIRST STORY KING WROTE AFTER HIS ACCIDENT.

immediately supported the idea and spent part of an afternoon setting up a temporary office ("a little nest") for him. "Tabitha Spruce of Oldtown [sic], Maine, knows when I'm working too hard, but she also knows that sometimes it's the work that bails me out,"[144] King wrote in *On Writing*.

Writing has always been the one constant in King's life, and during this personal crisis it was the best cure for his pain. He said that it was "very difficult to push the pen forty-five minutes a day, but it was vital to get back to work, because you have to break the ice somehow. You have to say, 'This is what I do.' I'm either going to continue to work, or I'm not. You say, 'If I can do this, maybe I can walk. If I can walk, maybe I can resume some kind of human intercourse.' Work seemed like a logical place to start."[145]

It would be trite to say that King's career can be divided into two phases, "before the accident" and "after the accident" (King and his wife call postaccident life "The Bonus Round"[146]), but the accident permeated much of his work in the ensuing years. He wrote about the incident in detail when he returned to *On Writing*. It was now part of who he was, another item in his C.V.

The first story he published in the aftermath was *Riding the Bullet*, a novella that took the publishing world by storm because of its unique delivery system—only available as a downloadable pdf. It is probably no coincidence that King chose to name the roller coaster featured in the story after Bryan Smith's Rottweiler.

His first postaccident novel, *Dreamcatcher*, was written between late 1999 and the middle of 2000 entirely by hand, using a Waterman cartridge fountain pen and tall hardcover ledgers. "To write the first draft of such a long book by hand put me in touch with the language as I haven't been for years," King reflects. "I even wrote one night (during a power outage) by

> "WRITING THE FIRST DRAFT OF SUCH A LONG BOOK BY HAND PUT ME IN TOUCH WITH THE LANGUAGE AS I HAVEN'T BEEN FOR YEARS."

candlelight. One rarely finds such opportunities in the twenty-first century, and they are to be savored."[147]

One of the four main characters in the novel, Jonesy, was struck by a car and has barely recovered enough to join his friends on their annual camping trip in western Maine. The sense of "before and after" is part of Jonesy's reality. Perhaps thinking about himself, King says, "It was as if there were two of him now, the one before he had been knocked flat in the street and the warier, older fellow who had awakened in Mass General." The character thinks of the version of himself from before the accident as "the whole Jonesy." He is a man in perpetual discomfort and pain, reflecting King's condition at the time he was working on the novel.

While writing *Kingdom Hospital*, a miniseries adaptation of Lars von Trier's movie *Riget* (which King had rented while in Colorado working on *The Shining* miniseries several years earlier), he included a grueling, detailed recreation of his own accident, complete with the offending van, its drug-addled driver, and his Rottweilers.

When he returned to work on the Dark Tower series in 2001, the accident became a central part of the plot. King's survival—and the very real possibility that he could have died that day without ever completing his magnum opus—became a Dark Tower of sorts.

Duma Key also features a character who is recovering from a catastrophic accident in which he was permanently maimed. Edgar Freemantle suffers from phantom pains in his lost limb—but he has gained something in return: the power to change reality through his paintings.

There is a popular belief that true art arises from misery or suffering. Whether or not that is true, King's muses were definitely influenced by the trauma he endured in 1999—and the pain he has suffered ever since.

11 MORE WORLDS THAN THESE

"THE WORLD HAD MOVED ON SINCE THEN.
THE WORLD HAD EMPTIED."

THE DARK TOWER SERIES

During King's *From a Buick 8* book tour, a fan in Dearborn, Michigan, told him, "Man, we heard about the accident, and the first thing we said is, 'The Dark Tower will never get finished now,'" to which King responded, "Thanks for the sympathy, guys."[148]

The Dark Tower stands at the nexus of not only this universe but *all* universes. The quest to keep the Tower from falling has been central to King's writing since the beginning, and yet the Dark Tower series stands apart from the rest of his work. Based on straw polls King occasionally conducted during public appearances, he came to the conclusion that half of his fans hadn't read the Dark Tower books.

King was only twenty-one years old when he wrote the famous opening line of the series: "The man in black fled across the desert, and the gunslinger followed." His inspirations were as diverse as the poetry of Robert Browning, the spaghetti westerns of Sergio Leone (starring Clint Eastwood, who many readers see as the gunslinger, Roland Deschain), and *Lord of the Rings*.

The five stories that comprise *The Gunslinger* were first published in *The Magazine of Fantasy and Science Fiction* between 1978 and 1981 before being collected in a limited edition of 10,000 copies published by a small press in Rhode Island. (It was the largest small-press edition in history at the time.) The book escaped the notice of most casual King fans until it was listed on the author's ad card at the front of *Pet Sematary* in 1983.

Fans bombarded King and his publisher with letters asking how to obtain a copy of this elusive book. King believed the story had limited appeal to his regular readers, but he underestimated their zeal—or their rancor when they learned the book was sold out. He authorized a second printing, but that did little to staunch demand. "It took the resulting flood of mail to make me uneasily aware that I had either wider responsibilities in the matter of my completed work, or people thought that I did," he said.[149]

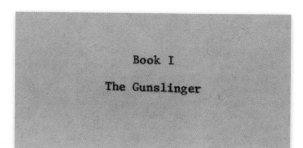

Book I

The Gunslinger

above TITLE PAGE FROM THE FIRST DRAFT OF THE GUNSLINGER, BOOK ONE OF THE DARK TOWER SERIES.

PHOTO OF KING TAKEN BY HIS BROTHER, DAVID, CIRCA 1967. A COPY OF STARTLING MYSTERY STORIES IS
PROPPED UP ON THE TYPEWRITER, OPEN TO THE TITLE PAGE OF HIS SHORT STORY "THE GLASS FLOOR."

Chapter I: The Desert

The man in black fled across the desert, and the gunslinger followed. The desert was the apotheosis of all deserts, huge, standing to the sky for what might have been parsecs in all directions; white; blinding; waterless; without feature save for the faint, cloudy haze of the mountains which sketched themselves on the horizon, the devil-grass which brought sweet dreams, nightmares, death; and the occasional leaning tombstone sign pointing the way. For once the drifted track that cut its way through the thick crust of alkali had been a road and coaches had followed it. The world had moved on since then. The world had emptied.

The gunslinger walked stolidly, not hurrying, not loafing. A hide waterbag was slung around his middle like a bloated sausage. It was almost full. He had progressed through the karma over many years, and had reached the fifth level. At seventh, or eighth, he would not have been thirsty; he could have watched his own body dehydrate with clinical, detached attention, watering its crevaces and dark inner hollows only when his mind told him it must be done. He was not seventh or eighth. He was fifth. So he was thirsty, although he had no particular urge to drink. In a vague way all this pleased him: it was romantic, therefore right.

Below the waterbag were his guns, finely weighted to his hand. The two belts crisscrossed above his crotch. The holsters were

Ultimately, King allowed the book to be published in paperback in 1988. Three more books in the series appeared over the next decade, *The Drawing of the Three* in 1987, *The Waste Lands* in 1992, and *Wizard and Glass* in 1997. King's determination to continue with the series was inspired in part by the ongoing demand from readers for new installments. One fan letter contained a Polaroid of a teddy bear in chains, with a message cut out of newspaper headlines. "'RELEASE THE NEXT *DARK TOWER* BOOK AT ONCE OR THE BEAR DIES,' it said. I put it up in my office to remind myself both of my responsibility and of how wonderful it is to have people actually care—a little—about the creatures of one's imagination."[150]

Usually, when King finds a story difficult going, he abandons it. He would have quit writing *The Stand* when he reached a seemingly intractable plotting crisis if he hadn't invested so much time in the book already, and he gave up on *The Plant* when he felt

Suddenly aware of his mortality, King decided to finish off the series once and for all. Starting in 2001, for sixteen months King worked on little else but the last three books, producing over 2,500 manuscript pages. He also revised *The Gunslinger*, which he felt tried too hard to be "something really, really important."[153] The unrelenting pace and the notion of finishing a lifelong work took its toll. Pleading exhaustion, he announced on his Web site in June 2002 that he was taking a one-month break to recharge his batteries. He was on a book tour when he started up again, but he timed his writing so that he would be back in Bangor, where he had started the first volume over thirty years earlier, when he finished the seventh and final book.

As he neared the end of the series, he told a reporter that he was ready to retire. "In a sense, once these [Dark Tower] books are done, there's nothing else to say."[154] He worried that his readers would think he was starting to repeat himself, that they would see *From a Buick 8* as a rehash of *Christine*, for example. "You can either continue to go on, or say I left when I was still on top of my game. I left when I was still holding the ball, instead of it holding me."[155] He said he wouldn't be able to stop writing "because I don't know what I'd do between nine and one every day," but he would just file the manuscripts away. "I don't need the money."[156]

He later dismissed his plans to retire as the words of someone who was exhausted from the epic writing journey he had just undergone.

like he was pushing the story instead of being pulled along by it. However, he kept going back to the story of the Dark Tower every five years or so, even though progress was difficult. In the afterword of the third book, he wrote, "Finding the doors to Roland's world has never been easy for me, and it seems to take more and more whittling to make each successive key fit each successive lock. Nevertheless . . . I still am able to find Roland's world when I set my wits to it, and it still holds me in thrall . . . more, in many ways, than any of the other worlds I have wandered in my imagination."[151]

Even when King wasn't writing Dark Tower novels, the series was percolating in the back of his mind. During the 1990s, the mythos began to intrude more and more into his other novels, books like *Rose Madder*, *Insomnia*, *Desperation*, and *Hearts in Atlantis*. When Peter Straub suggested that they add Dark Tower elements to their collaborative novel *Black House*, King replied, "I don't know if I can keep it out. At this point, everything I write is connected to it."[152]

The Dark Tower series unifies much of King's fiction. "I am coming to understand that Roland's world (or worlds) actually contains all the others of my making," he once said.[157] A popular game among fans is looking for connections among King's various books. When Roland and his followers escape from an insane monorail, they find themselves in a world very much like the one readers know from *The Stand*. Characters such as Father Callahan (*'Salem's Lot*), Randall Flagg (*The Stand*), Ted Brautigan (*Hearts in Atlantis*), and Patrick Danville (*Insomnia*) all make their curtain calls within the series.

above FIRST EDITION HARDCOVER OF THE DARK TOWER: THE GUNSLINGER, PUBLISHED BY DONALD M. GRANT, A SMALL PRESS LOCATED IN RHODE ISLAND.

EARLY 1980s-ERA CONTACT STRIPS. SINCE KING IS SPORTING A BEARD, THE PHOTOS MUST HAVE BEEN TAKEN SOME TIME AFTER THE END OF THE WORLD SERIES AND BEFORE THE BEGINNING OF SPRING TRAINING.

CONTACT STRIPS, EARLY 1980s ERA.

ENCLOSED

MANUSCRIPT Four hand-edited pages from "The Slow Mutants" section of a manuscript of *The Dark Tower: The Gunslinger.* The first four books were published without the benefit of professional copyediting, so numerous mistakes crept into the story. Some of them King later explained using his concept of parallel universes. However, the sentence he inserted on page 8 where Roland asks about movies did not make it into the final manuscript, but the word "again" further down the page did, which surely confused some readers.

SKETCH This sketch was found sandwiched between two pages of the first draft manuscript for *The Drawing of the Three.* The artist is unknown.

LEDGER This handwritten ledger contains a section of an unpublished story called "Muffe" that has the feel of the Dark Tower. Part of Chapter 17, Section 11 from *Needful Things*; some notes from King to himself about the story (he calls these "Needful Thoughts"); and a part of Chapter 5 of *Insomnia* that is substantially different from the published version.

As he began to turn, a club crashed down on Roland's shoulder, numbing his right arm all the way to the wrist. He held onto the gun and fired once the bullet went into one of the wagon-wheels, s a wooden spoke and turning the wheel on its hub with high screeing sound. Behind him, he heard the green folk in the street uttering hoarse, yapping cries as they charged forward.

Steve — your use of scree as for sounds is not supported by my big dictionary — see OED

One of the prevailing themes in King's books and stories is that reality is thin, and there are countless, perhaps infinite, parallel universes adjacent to one another. The zealous driver in his short story "Mrs. Todd's Shortcut" knew this, finding faster routes to her destinations by cutting through from one dimension to the next. Jack Sawyer in *The Talisman* did much the same thing. The mysterious car in *From a Buick 8* acted as a portal into another reality, and Scott Landon jumped to a place he called Boo'ya Moon when things got tough in *Lisey's Story*. In the novella *N.* (from *Just After Sunset*), King again explored the notion of the thin curtain between parallel realities ("thinnies" he calls such places) and what might happen if things moved from one dimension to another. In "Ur," an e-book reader becomes a portal to other worlds.

The extension of this philosophy of the multiverse is the notion that something binds these parallel realities all together, an axis around which they all rotate in the space-time continuum. This is the Dark Tower, which has different representations in the myriad universes—in the worlds of Eddie, Jake, and Susannah, it is a pink rose in a vacant lot.

The epic fantasy of the Dark Tower series, blended with the feel of a classic western and elements of horror and science fiction, is ultimately a tale of good versus evil. Roland and his followers (his "ka-tet") represent the white, supported by a mysterious force known as "ka" that wants them to succeed. The opposing force, the red, is led by the Crimson King and his minions, including Randall Flagg. Roland's goal is to preserve reality, while the Crimson

AUDIO KING

Most of King's novels are available in unabridged audio versions. There are a few exceptions: classic novels such as *The Stand* and *It* are not yet available in commercial form, although they have been recorded for the visually impaired audience.

King recorded the audio versions of the first three Dark Tower novels himself, making use of the studio at WZON, the radio station he owns in Bangor. Careful listeners can hear traffic sounds—transports, especially—in the background of these early recordings. For subsequent books, professional narrators were hired, including George Guidall and Ron McLarty.

Frank Muller was one of the most popular readers, an award-winning stage actor who had his own recording studio at home and narrated the works of many authors, including John le Carré, John Grisham, and Elmore Leonard. After Muller was incapacitated following a motorcycle accident, King helped establish a charity for performing artists without health insurance.

More recently, King narrated *Bag of Bones* and first-person sections of *Hearts in Atlantis*. Actors such as Sissy Spacek, Kathy Bates, James Woods, Frances Sternhagen, John Hurt, Anne Heche, and Mare Winningham, several of whom have also appeared in movie adaptations of his novels, have also narrated his novels and short stories.

King wants to topple the Dark Tower so he can rule the resulting chaos.

The Dark Tower series has parallels in *The Wizard of Oz*. Roland's ka-tet consists of broken people—a junkie, a legless woman with multiple personality disorder, a neglected young boy, an ostracized but intelligent animal—who are striving to better themselves while at the same time trying to make it back home to the realities from which Roland has plucked them.

On another level, the series is about the act of writing. Because the early novels weren't copyedited before publication, mistakes crept in. Some were simple errors in geography; others were continuity errors between the books. Characters' names and ages changed. King incorporated these errors into the books, suggesting that they weren't mistakes but rather details from nearly parallel but slightly different realities. Eddie's sister might have been named Selina in one reality and Gloria in another, perhaps the one where the story of *The Shining* was so important that it needed to exist, even if Stephen King didn't write it.

King, too, is a pawn of ka. In the keystone reality, a fictionalized version of himself is writing the story of Roland's quest while the Crimson King conspires to stop him. By inserting himself into his magnum opus, King enters the realm of metafiction (a "smarmy academic term" that King says he hates[158]), fiction that comments directly on the nature of writing and the act of creation. He uses the story to examine aspects of his career and his life, although he has the freedom to take liberties with any of those details since this is, after all, fiction.

The series explores some of the profound questions of existence. Roland is a tool of the universe, but an imperfect one: strong and determined enough to fulfill his destiny but sufficiently flawed that he fails at his personal goal, which is to not simply save the Tower but to conquer it, to enter within and discover for himself the nature of reality. King seems to say that Roland's hubris—his desire to know that which humanity is not meant to know—is his curse, and that only when he is able to free himself of this desire will he truly succeed.

right A "FICTIONALIZED VERSION" OF STEPHEN KING.

King has had a lifelong relationship with Randall Flagg. In 1969, he wrote a poem called "The Dark Man" on the back of a placemat in a diner. Later published in *Ubris* and *Moth*, two University of Maine literary magazines, the poem tells of a man who wanders the country like a vagabond, riding the rails, observing everything. It turns dark when the narrator confesses to rape and murder.

> *a savage sacrifice*
>
> *and a sign to those who creep in*
>
> *fixed ways:*
>
> *i am a dark man.*[159]

King later said, "[T]hat idea of the guy never left my mind. The thing about him that really attracted me was the idea of the villain as somebody who was always on the outside looking in and hated people who had good fellowship and good conversation and friends."[160] His obsession with Flagg may have originated with Charlie Starkweather. As a boy, King kept a scrapbook about the man who went on a killing spree with his underage girlfriend in 1958. He wanted to familiarize himself with the blank look he detected in Starkweather's face and avoid people if he saw that same look again.

Flagg appeared in *The Stand* and again in *The Eyes of the Dragon*. Characters with the same initials pop up in other books—Raymond Fiegler in *Hearts in Atlantis*, for example. Though it took King a while to arrive at this conclusion, the man in black who Roland Deschain chases across the desert in *The Gunslinger* proved to be another incarnation of Flagg named Walter o'Dim.

Despite the fact that he causes chaos wherever he appears, Flagg's fiendish plots almost always end in failure. Nearly thirty-five years after the dark man materialized in King's mind at that diner, Flagg met his fate at the hands of one of his own creations, Mordred Deschain, in *The Dark Tower*, a victim of his own hubris.

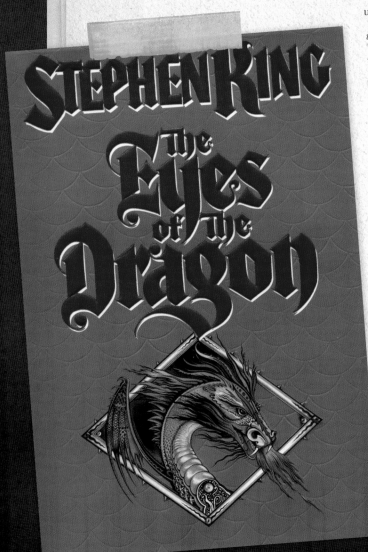

VIKING PENGUIN HARDCOVER OF *THE EYES OF THE DRAGON* (1987).

THE DARK MAN

"Let us go, then, you and I..."
T. S. Eliot

i have stridden the fuming way
of sun-hammered tracks and
smashed cinders;
i have ridden rails
and burned sterno in the
gantry silence of hobo jungles;
i am a dark man.

i have ridden rails
and passed the smuggery
of desperate houses with counterfeit chimneys
and heard from the outside
the inside clink of cocktail ice
while closed doors broke the world—
and over it all a savage sickle moon
that bummed my eyes with bones of light.

i have slept in glaring swamps
where mush-reek rose
to mix with the sex smell of
rotting cypress stumps
where witch fire clung in sunken
psycho spheres of baptism—
and heard the suck of shadows
where a gutted columned house
leeched with vines
speaks to an overhung mushroom sky.

i have fed dimes to cold machines
in all night filling stations
while traffic in a mad and flowing flame
streaked red in six lanes of darkness,
and breathed the cleaver hitckhike wind
within the breakdown lane with thumb levelled
and saw shadowed faces made complacent
with heaters behind safety glass
faces that rose like complacent moons
in the undulent shadow of all this monster void.

and in the sudden flash of hate and lonely
cold as the center of a sun
i forced a girl in a field of wheat
and left her sprawled with the virgin bread
a savage sacrifice
and a sign to those who creep in
fixed ways:
i am a dark man.

— Steve King

KING'S POEM "THE DARK MAN" (LEFT), WHICH
HE HAS IDENTIFIED AS THE GENESIS FOR THE
CHARACTER RANDALL FLAGG, APPEARED IN THE
FALL 1969 EDITION OF UBRIS (ABOVE), A UNIVERSITY
OF MAINE LITERARY MAGAZINE.

12

THE THING WITH THE ENDLESS PIEBALD SIDE

"EACH MARRIAGE HAS TWO HEARTS, ONE LIGHT AND ONE DARK."

LISEY'S STORY

In *Misery*, when Paul Sheldon completed *Fast Cars*, he congratulated himself by thinking that he might have just won next year's American Book Award. Johnny Marinville in *Desperation* is a National Book Award winner and was once "spoken of in connection with the Nobel Prize for Literature." Mid-list author Mike Noonan (*Bag of Bones*) never won any awards, but Scott Landon (*Lisey's Story*) has won both the Pulitzer and the National Book Award—and a World Fantasy Award, too.

Critical opinion toward Stephen King has changed over the years. *Time* magazine called him the "Master of Post-Literate Prose" after the release of *Different Seasons*. King famously called himself "the literary equivalent of a Big Mac and fries," a self-effacing quote that will follow him to the grave. However, the establishment started taking him more seriously after his work appeared in literary magazines such as *The New Yorker*, *The Paris Review*, and *McSweeney's*.

He is the recipient of Bram Stoker Awards, World Fantasy Awards, International Horror Guild Awards, British Fantasy Association Awards, and a Hugo, to name but a few. He has been recognized for a lifetime of achievement by the Horror Writers Association, the Mystery Writers of America, the World Fantasy Convention, and the Canadian Booksellers Association—the first non-Canadian to receive this honor. His short story "The Man in the Black Suit" won a prestigious O. Henry Award in 1996—although he says he is "convinced someone had made a mistake"[161] and speculated that the only reason he won was because his name appeared nowhere on the story when it was presented to the judges.

His highest accolade to date, though, came in 2003 when he was awarded the Medal for Distinguished Contribution to American Letters from the National Book Foundation, a controversial decision. King was delighted and surprised to learn that he had won. He said, "It takes a certain amount of courage to give that sort of award to a popular writer, because this automatic prejudice kicks in where there's a mindset that says, 'If millions of people are reading this guy, he really can't be any good.'"[162]

King wasn't the first popular author to win the award—it had previously been given to Ray Bradbury—but there was something about him winning that riled the literary establishment. King welcomed the debate in his acceptance speech, saying, "The people who speak out, speak out because they are passionate about the book, about the word, about the page and, in that sense, we're all brothers and sisters."[163]

right KING HOLDS UP HIS LIFETIME ACHIEVEMENT AWARD FROM THE CANADIAN BOOKSELLERS ASSOCIATION IN TORONTO, ONTARIO, JUNE 8, 2007. HE WAS THE FIRST NON-CANADIAN TO RECEIVE THE AWARD.

His speech was primarily a love letter to his wife Tabitha. However, he took advantage of the spotlight to chastise people who took pride in the fact that they hadn't read popular writers like John Grisham, Tom Clancy, Mary Higgins Clark, Jack Ketchum, or Peter Straub. "What do you think? You get social or academic brownie points for deliberately staying out of touch with your own culture?"[164]

What the audience didn't know on that November evening in 2003 was that the award meant so much to King that he literally risked his life to accept the medal and deliver his speech. The lung that had been punctured by one of his ribs in 1999 hadn't healed properly, leading to a serious case of pneumonia. His doctors had advised against attending the banquet—they wanted him to go straight to the hospital. Instead, King put on a brave face and masked his discomfort. The next day he entered the hospital, where he stayed for nearly two months. It was the second time that the van accident almost killed him.

While he was in the hospital, his wife decided to redecorate his home studio. He remembers, "When I came back, she said, 'I wouldn't go in there; it's disturbing.' So of course I went in there, and it was disturbing. . . . [T]he furniture had been pulled out because my wife was getting it reupholstered, and the rugs had been rolled up. I thought, This is what this place is going to look like after I die. . . . When I thought of my wife cleaning out my papers, a light went on. *Lisey's Story* bloomed from that."[165]

It took a while to recover from his prolonged hospitalization, but he started on the novel right away. "I was just nauseated all the time. I couldn't keep food down. I felt like crap. The book was just angelic . . . I actually literally wrote *Lisey* in between running to the bathroom to vomit what I had eaten last."[166]

King originally intended for *Lisey's Story* to be a funny book about the spouse of a famous writer. "I wanted to show that his wife got completely ignored, but was the person responsible for all his success," he said. "I wanted to have five or six things in the background where she had actually pulled all his chestnuts out of the fire. Then this guy Dooley came on the scene and wanted the writer's manuscripts and the story took a different direction. It got more serious."[167]

Bag of Bones and *Lisey's Story* form bookends—in the former, the writer has to learn how to survive in the aftermath of his wife's death, while in the latter, the opposite is true. In a sense, Lisey Landon isn't really a widow yet, because she's still living as if her husband Scott were with her. Two years after his death, Scott's office looks like he could walk in at any moment, sit at his desk and start writing again. His voice is alive in her head and his untouched office is a metaphor for her suppressed grief.

She's finally decided that it's time to pack up certain things, figure out what to do with all of his books and papers, and move on. King isn't interested in writing about death itself. He says, "I think that we pretty much wink out, that we're gone. When we die, that's it, and if there's an afterlife it's so hypothetical that it almost doesn't bear thinking about as a writer. What does interest me is what happens to love in the wake of death and how it lasts."[168]

King creates such an intimate depiction of a long, successful marriage—with its private language, inside jokes, and almost telepathic communication—that his wife worried readers would assume he was writing about their life. He took pains to delineate the differences during his publicity tour for the book, saying, "Scott and Lisey are not me and Tabby. We have been married a long time, but unlike Lisey, Tabby did

> "I THINK THAT WE PRETTY MUCH WINK OUT, THAT WE'RE GONE. WHEN WE DIE, THAT'S IT. . . . WHAT DOES INTEREST ME IS WHAT HAPPENS TO LOVE IN THE WAKE OF DEATH AND HOW IT LASTS."

left STEPHEN AND TABITHA KING AT THE 54TH ANNUAL NATIONAL BOOK AWARDS CEREMONY AND BENEFIT DINNER IN MANHATTAN ON NOVEMBER 19, 2003. KING'S ACCEPTANCE SPEECH WAS IN LARGE PART A LOVE LETTER TO HIS WIFE.

graduate from college, and she's written books of her own, and they're good ones. Scott and Lisey are childless, and we have three wonderful kids that are no longer kids and are all grown up."[169]

Instead of using his regular editor, Chuck Verrill, King handed the first draft manuscript over to Nan Graham, the editor in chief at Scribner. He is very aware of the popular conception that authors like him who sell a lot of books are immune to being edited. He rebuffed that notion, saying, "To those tempted to say that about *Lisey's Story*, I would be happy to submit sample pages from my first-draft manuscript, complete with Nan's notes. I had first-year French essays that came back cleaner."[170]

The novel spans about a week of contemporary time and a quarter of a century of history. Scott and Lisey's love story rolls out in reverse. Lisey has forgotten some details of her marriage and there were facts about her husband's past that she never knew. King says, "The book is a celebration of monogamy, in a way. It is also about how even in the most intimate relationships we are always holding something back."[171]

HAROLD BLOOM ON STEPHEN KING

Harold Bloom, Yale University's Sterling Professor of Humanities has been described as the (self-proclaimed) defender of the literary canon.[172] He is not Stephen King's number one fan. Not even number one hundred and one.

In his introduction to a volume he edited containing essays analyzing King's works, Bloom admits his disdain for his subject. "I will confine this brief Introduction to just two of King's works, *Carrie* and *The Shining*, equally famous, and clearly representative of his achievement, whatever that is. With great effort, I have just reread both." (He also later professed to having "suffered a great deal" while reading one of J. K. Rowling's novels). He says, "The narrative line of each book has a certain coherence and drive; the prose is undistinguished, and there is nothing much that could be termed characterization or inwardness, or even vivid caricature."

He concludes that "I cannot locate any aesthetic dignity in King's writing . . . King will be remembered as a sociological phenomenon, an image of the death of the Literate Reader."[173] Given his feelings on the matter, one wonders why he was editing a book that treated King as a valid subject of critical analysis.

Five years later, when the National Book Foundation bestowed upon King their medal for Distinguished Contribution to American Letters, Bloom was sufficiently incensed to write an op-ed piece for the *Los Angeles Times*. Calling King a writer of "penny dreadfuls," he declared the decision "another low in the shocking process of dumbing down our cultural life . . . What he is is an immensely inadequate writer, on a sentence-by-sentence, paragraph-by-paragraph, book-by-book basis."[174]

STEPHEN KING ON HAROLD BLOOM

"Harold Bloom has never been very interested in popular culture, and he has no real grasp of popular culture, popular writing, or the places where what we call pop culture crosses what you would call higher culture . . . What I would really like to do is see Harold Bloom given an injection of sodium pentothal so that he had to tell the truth and say, 'Now, Harold, how much Stephen King have you actually read?' And I think that the answer would be probably less than one whole book. My guess is he's dipped a few times, and you come to the table with certain prejudices, and naturally you're going to see those prejudices fulfilled."[175]

"I'm just a creature of my culture, and there are people who've damned me for that. Harold Bloom is one of them. He's described me as desperately inadequate, but then there are people who see the culture itself as desperately inadequate. I think that if you love Stephen King you'll love the culture and if you hate Stephen King you probably hate the culture."[176]

king's garbage truck

by Steve King

The Goddard College Dancers, seven students from a small liberal arts school in Vermont, put on a program called *Why We Dance* last Sunday night in Hauck Auditorium. Attendence was lackluster—nothing new—but the two or three hundred who did attend caught an astonishing potpourri of modern and folk dance that ranged from the very good to the astonishingly awful.

The bad was the final act, a three-part impression of an accident looking for someplace to happen, called *North East Passing*. Choreographed by Yvonne Rainer, *Passing* showed no particular form, artistry, theme, or merit of any kind. Someone should find Miss Rainer and send her back to dancing school.

But the good was very good, the best being a terrifying piece called *Child of Our Darkness*, choreographed by Ann Ryder and featuring Wynde Winston and John Caldwell, the only male in the troupe. Miss Winston, portraying a child-woman torn between forces of light and darkness, was very good indeed. The conclusion, with burning flames projected onto her body and a screen behind her was almost numbing in impact—a Joan of Arc for our times, perhaps.

The three folk dances presented were also interesting—the best being the American folk dance, Genevieve McClelland and Wynde Winston gyrating with a kind of expressionless abandon to the sexual electronic rhythms of the Butterfield Blues Band singing "Good Morning Little School-Girl."

They were good, they were enthusiastic, they communicated. At times they seemed a bit too careful, at times their material was bad, but on the whole the Goddard College Dancers made it. You people who weren't in the empty seats are culturally deprived.

If you're not doing anything interesting Friday night, February 28th, go on upstairs to Hauck Auditorium and catch the movie. You may go home with gray hair, but that's okay. You won't notice. You'll be too busy trying to persuade your girl to walk *you* home.

The movie is *Hush . . . Hush, Sweet Charlotte*, and if you think you saw it on TV, you're wrong. What you saw was *Charlotte* cut to ribbons by smarty-pants ABC censors who would probably like to see Halloween outlawed. If you saw it in the movies, go see it again. As Judith Crist likes to say, go back and savor it.

The thing to savor is Bette Davis as Charlotte, looking like a malevolent Shirley Temple in her bangs and puffy-armed white dresses. Miss Davis is pushing sixty-five by now, still smokes three packs of Luckies a day, swears like a drill sergeant, and can scare the hell out of you before you can say Witch Hazel. She has a voice like an electric drill somebody left out in the rain, and she really puts it to use in the near-climactic scene when she discovers Joseph Cotten, whom she thought she had murdered, at the top of the stairs. Bette crawls slowly down that shadowy, decayed stairway letting out the most godawful sounds you have ever heard. Mary Poppins she ain't, but then, I have a feeling she could eat Julie Andrews for dinner with Dick Van Dyke for dessert.

Agnes Moorehead is excellent as the maid, Joseph Cotten fairly good as the doctor (although I keep expecting him to drag out a bottle of Aspirin and launch into his spiel), and Olivia DeHavilland is at least passable as Charlotte's cousin.

If you're big on spooky movies go see it. Even if you're not, Bette Davis is one of the best, and she may not be around much longer, especially at three packs a day.

Since 2003, King has been writing a column called "The Pop of King" for *Entertainment Weekly* magazine. In it he discusses pop culture—primarily movies, television books, and music, with occasional forays into more controversial topics like politics and movie snacks.

This isn't King's first gig addressing pop culture. From early 1969 until his graduation from the University of Maine, he wrote a weekly column called "King's Garbage Truck" for the *Maine Campus*. He wrote about TV game shows, movies, the Beatles, baseball, birth control, the pressures of being a student, and campus and global politics.

While he lived in Colorado in 1974, he sent a query letter to the *Boulder Daily Camera* hoping to get a job writing entertaining movie reviews for the paper. "I don't want to write snotty avant-garde reviews of obscure foreign films," he wrote. "And by the way, I work cheap."

THE FIRST "KING'S GARBAGE TRUCK" COLUMN, FEBRUARY 20, 1969.

Before he died, Scott prepared one last "Bool Hunt," a game he and his brother invented to help them survive their father's "bad gunky," a dangerous mania that overtook him from time to time. The scavenger hunt, designed to "allow her to face in stages something she couldn't face all at once," is part of Lisey's healing process, like cleaning out Scott's office. Once she rediscovers all the things she's forgotten and learns the truth of her husband's childhood, she can get past her grief.

Like the Kings, the Landons started out poor, which enhanced their intimacy in the early years. It was them against the world. Scott had no living relatives. Lisey, on the other hand, came from a sprawling family of sisters.

Because of Scott's tortured past, he refuses to have children—it's the one deal breaker that Lisey must accept if she wants a life with him. It's the only way he knows that will break his family's cycle of violence. As Scott's career took off, he turned into a bona fide celebrity and Lisey fell into his shadow, in public at least. In private, she was the stable ground on which their marriage was built, helping to keep Scott's inherited madness in check.

Scott has an enormous fan base that includes crazies (Deep Space Cowboys, he calls them) who want to do him harm, like the guy who shoots him during a groundbreaking ceremony for a university library. Par for the course, Lisey's role in saving her

husband's life that day went unheralded. She sometimes amuses herself by finding identifiable parts of her body—a knee here, a purse there—in media photographs of her famous husband, where she is often acknowledged only as his "gal pal."

The book revisits King's belief that reality is thin. Boo'ya Moon, where Scott goes when he is injured, is a close kin to the Territories from *The Talisman*. It is also the source of Scott's literary inspiration, the "myth pool" that is part of the collective unconscious to which writers have special access, a term King learned from his university professor Burton Hatlen. King said once in an interview, "Imagination is a wonderful thing, but it's also a terrible thing. . . . It's sweet in the daytime and awful at night."[177]

King also explores the concept of an author's literary legacy. Academics and fans would love to get their hands on any unpublished manuscripts Scott left behind. Lisey calls these people "incunks," a corruption of "incunabula," a word that refers to the earliest printed documents. The most ardent incunk, Joseph Woodbury, a professor from Scott's alma mater, sends a crazed and violent fan to underscore his interest in Scott's ephemera.

All of these challenges are part of what makes this Lisey's story; she steps out from the shadow of her husband's fame and the almost oppressive weight of their now-absent relationship to become a strong woman who can not only provide support for her ailing sister but also face the seemingly relentless forces that have aligned against her.

Lisey's Story is King's most personal novel, a mature reflection on his long and successful marriage, his equally long and spectacularly successful writing career, and his ruminations on what might happen after he's gone. It's a book that could only have been written by someone who has lived a full life and is now shifting his focus to encompass the clearing at the end of the path.

above During a November 9, 2006, press conference in London for the UK launch of Lisey's Story, King announced that he had discovered a new Richard Bachman novel, titled Blaze.

THE INNOVATOR

Over the years, King has experimented with nontraditional forms of publication. Though *Riding the Bullet* made headlines when he released the novella only as a download, that wasn't his first experiment with Internet publishing.

In 1993, King made his short story "Umney's Last Case" available over the Internet several weeks prior to its appearance in *Nightmares and Dreamscapes*. This was before Web browsers were a fixture of every home computer and before the standardization of document formats. People who paid a $5 fee could use an FTP service to log into a remote computer and download the story, which came bundled with a program that displayed the text onscreen.

With *The Plant*, King tested the theory that most people are honest. Six installments of the novel-in-progress were made available on his Web site on the honor system. If a large enough percentage of people who downloaded the files contributed a dollar, he promised to continue with the project. Despite respectable returns (he called the experiment "permission to print money"), payment percentages started to fall with later installments. Before the numbers were tabulated, though, he discovered that the story wasn't working for him and abandoned the project. Pundits erroneously cited *The Plant* as an example of a failed experiment in Web publishing when, in fact, it was just another failed novel.

In recent years, King has entered into the burgeoning world of graphic novels, with adaptations of his Dark Tower series, *The Stand*, and *The Talisman* in progress. Over a million people viewed the animated graphic adaptation of his novella *N.* from *Just After Sunset*.

He is considering doing a YouTube video as part of the promotional campaign for *Under the Dome*, and he recently released a novella for—and inspired by—the Kindle book reader.

KING'S RECENT NOVELLA UR, ABOUT A PINK KINDLE THAT COULD ACCESS NEWS AND BOOKS FROM ALTERNATE REALITIES, WAS RELEASED EXCLUSIVELY FOR THE AMAZON E-BOOK READER.

STEPHEN KING: SPORTSWRITER

Stephen King's affinity for baseball is no secret. He is one of the Boston Red Sox's biggest fans, often seen in the stands at their games, usually with a book in hand to read between innings. For many years, he shaved off his beard at the beginning of spring training and put his razor away after the World Series.

His characters are usually Red Sox fans—as early as in the 1975 short story "The Lawnmower Man." In the Dark Tower series, both Father Callahan and John Cullum ask Eddie Dean if the Red Sox ever win the World Series in their futures; these are men contemplating the fate of the universe, but they still find time to talk baseball.

King's first appearance in *The New Yorker* was a 1990 essay called "Head Down" that chronicles the 1989 season of his son Owen's Little League baseball team, which won the state championship that year. In the introduction to *Nightmares and Dreamscapes*, King says that he "probably worked harder on it than anything else I've written over the last fifteen years."

He used a Red Sox pitcher as the title character in *The Girl Who Loved Tom Gordon* and had the good fortune to chronicle a Red Sox season in *Faithful* with co-author Stewart O'Nan during the year when the team broke their infamous World Series drought.

King's association with sports began at an early age. After getting in trouble for a parody of his teachers, his high school guidance councilor recommended him for a position at the *Lisbon Weekly Enterprise*. His experience under the hand of an astute and perceptive editor was a pivotal experience for King. The editor, John Gould, was responsible for a philosophy of writing that governed the rest of King's career: write with the door closed, rewrite with the door open.

When King threw the opening pitch at a game at Fenway in 2004, the *Boston Globe* blamed King for jinxing the Red Sox when they lost that night, ending a ten-game winning streak.

FENWAY PARK, OCTOBER 16, 2004. "THE GREAT THING ABOUT BASEBALL IS THAT YOU CAN GET EIGHTEEN PAGES READ JUST IN THE INNING BREAKS," KING ONCE TOLD A SPORTS REPORTER FROM FSN.

TAMPA BAY DEVIL RAYS PLAYERS STUCK PINS INTO KING'S AUTHOR PHOTO FROM A COPY OF <u>MISERY</u> IN AN ATTEMPT TO
END A LOSING STREAK THAT STARTED WHEN KING ATTENDED A MINNESOTA TWINS-DEVIL RAYS GAME IN 2002.

CONCLUSION
THE TEST OF TIME

"I SENSE STRONGLY THAT THIS WORLD IS A THIN PLACE INDEED, SIMPLY A VEIL OVER A BRIGHTER AND MORE AMAZING TRUTH." — STEPHEN KING

Some people believe that it is possible to learn about a writer through a careful reading of his or her work. Others think that a writer's work is best understood by knowing the details and circumstances of that person's life. Which way does the mirror point—or does it work in both directions?

Using King's racquetball metaphor, the events described in this book can be seen as the bricks that make up the wall that roots his fiction in reality. The previous chapters demonstrate how many of King's books were inspired—at least in part—by what was going on in his life at the time.

Though ideas for books can originate anywhere—a personal experience, overheard conversation, a news item, a dream—the stories arising from these ideas that resonate the strongest are the ones that are informed by real life. King establishes a close bond with his readers by incorporating his astute observations about people and daily life into his stories. Readers identify with his characters, even those that are caught up in circumstances well beyond human experience. People aren't likely to encounter a ghost or a vampire or a possessed car, but if they did, they would probably react in the ways that King describes in his books.

To King, one of the most important things a writer has to do is tell the truth—even when he's making things up.

Of course, this isn't the end of the story. Stephen King is still writing. Despite his occasional talk about retiring, either from writing or simply from publishing, it doesn't appear that he has any plans to slow down. In fact, his newest book, *Under the Dome,* is one of the longest of his career.

In the late 1990s, the Kings began wintering in Florida. In the past, King's relocations usually provided inspiration for new material. The year he lived in Boulder brought about Colorado-based novels like *The Shining*, *The Stand*, and *Misery*. It took a while longer for Florida to work its magic. While he knew he would ultimately write stories set there, he took his time. "You have to get a little bit of texture for a place," he told attendees of a writers' conference at Florida's Eckerd College in 2006.

His winter home first showed its influence in the short story "Rest Stop," published in *Esquire* in 2003. In 2006, he started work on *Duma Key*, his first novel set in Florida, and other stories in recent years—"The Gingerbread Girl" and "A Very Tight Place," both included in his most recent collection *Just After Sunset*—are also set in that state.

right READING A PAPERBACK COPY OF ALL THE KING'S MEN ON A STREET CORNER IN BANGOR.

King's office in Bangor, featuring fan art and movie memorabilia. The large painting on the floor was created by Drew Struzan for the movie adaptation of <u>The Mist</u>.

An intricately carved, one-of-a-kind Jack-in-the-Box, a gift from a fan, is prominently displayed on King's desk.

An entry by a finalist in a contest held by King's UK publisher to create a promotional poster for Duma Key.

THE GHOST BROTHERS OF DARKLAND COUNTY

For several years, Stephen King and musician John Mellencamp have been collaborating on *The Ghost Brothers of Darkland County*. It's not a traditional musical, but rather a dramatic play with music. Mellencamp has written well over a dozen songs for the project in styles ranging from jazz to blues to bluegrass to country to zydeco.

Mellencamp told King about a legend associated with a lake house he purchased in Indiana where a man shot his brother in a drunken game in the 1950s. The man and a girl ran into a tree while taking the injured brother to the hospital. All three died and their ghosts reportedly haunt the place.

King turned the concept into a more complex tale. A man takes his two sons— who hate each other—on vacation to a haunted cabin in Mississippi where his two older brothers and a beautiful young girl died forty years earlier as a result of sibling rivalry. What really happened that night is known only to the surviving brother, who witnessed everything.

The Ghost Brothers of Darkland County, which has been described as "a musical that men will enjoy," may premiere in the 2009–2010 season and, if successful, will move to Broadway.

That's not to say that King has abandoned Maine. *Under the Dome* is set in western Maine. The novel is a third stab at a story idea that he worked on in the 1980s, "which concerns itself with how people behave when they are cut off from the society they've always belonged to."[178] One incarnation of the book, set in an apartment building, was called *The Cannibals*. However, King ignored any previous work on the concept and started from scratch when tackling the story again in 2007.

"It isn't like a worldwide apocalypse or anything like that, but it's a very long book, and it deals with some of the same issues that *The Stand* does, but in a more allegorical way," King says of *Under the Dome*.[179]

After spending a year reading for his role as co-editor of *The Best American Short Stories*, he rediscovered the short form and has published several in recent years, including his first collaboration with his son Joe. His works are being reimagined as graphic novels. He is working with John Mellencamp to get *The Ghost Brothers of Darkland County* ready for its theatrical debut. He's writing regularly for *Entertainment Weekly*.

What will King's legacy be? He admits that he doesn't know, but he does have a vision of how he'd like to be remembered: "I think [people fifty years from now] will have some vague memory of my works and some of the older ones will have read it, and maybe some of the books will last. . . . You never know what's going to happen. . . . I think any writer would like to be remembered and be somebody who's read, you know, somebody whose work stands the test of time, so to speak. But on the other hand, as a person, I'll be dead, and if there's no afterlife then I won't give a shit, I'm gone. And if there is an afterlife I got an idea that what goes on here is a very minor concern. But you know, I'm built a certain way and the way I'm built is to try and give people pleasure. That's what I do. I want people to read the books and be knocked out and I'd like that to continue even after I stop."[180]

right PUBLICITY PHOTO BY AMY GUIP THAT APPEARED ON THE DUST JACKET OF LISEY'S STORY.

SELECTED BIBLIOGRAPHY

Danse Macabre, Stephen King, Everett House, 1981. In addition to being a compendium of the best in horror movies and novels, it contains "An Annoying Autobiographical Pause," among the earliest autobiographical writings by King.

Stephen King: The Art of Darkness, by Douglas E. Winter, New American Library, 1984. This was the first extensive examination of King and his works. Winter had full access to King and, while limited to the first decade of King's publishing career, this book remains one of the best combinations of biography and literary criticism.

Bare Bones: Conversations on Terror with Stephen King, Tim Underwood and Chuck Miller, editors, McGraw-Hill, 1988. The first of two books that reprint interviews King granted during the previous decade. Most of these interviews were never widely circulated before their appearance in these volumes.

Feast of Fear: Conversations with Stephen King, Tim Underwood and Chuck Miller, editors, Carroll & Graf, 1992. The second collection of interviews, some dating back as far as 1973.

Secret Windows, Stephen King, Book-of-the-Month Club, 2000. Released as a companion to *On Writing*, this is a collection of essays and book introductions by King, along with a few works of short fiction, including two juvenile stories from *Dave's Rag*, the newspaper his brother published in 1959–1960.

On Writing, Stephen King, Scribner, 2000. A combination of autobiography and advice for writers. In the "C.V." section, King outlines his credentials for the latter, an entertaining and insightful look at his writing career and personal history.

The Complete Stephen King Universe, Stanley Wiater, Christopher Golden, and Hank Wagner, St. Martin's Griffin, 2006. An updated version of their 2001 book, which tracks the connections among all of King's works, the ways in which his plots and characters intertwine.

Haunted Heart: The Life and Times of Stephen King, Lisa Rogak, Thomas Dunne Books, 2009. An unauthorized biography that pieces together events in King's life based on previous writings, extensive research, and new interviews with people who have been associated with King over the years, including the author of this book.

ABOUT THE AUTHOR

BEV VINCENT is a contributing editor with *Cemetery Dance* magazine, where he has been writing the column "News From the Dead Zone" since 2001. His first book, *The Road to the Dark Tower*, was nominated for a Bram Stoker Award in 2004. He co-edited *The Illustrated Stephen King Trivia Book* and has published over fifty short stories. His screenplay for the "dollar baby" film *Stephen King's Gotham Café*, co-written with two other writers, was named Best Adaptation at the International Horror and Sci-Fi Film Festival in 2004. His Web site is www.bevvincent.com.

ACKNOWLEDGMENTS

The people at becker&mayer! have been a delight to work with from this project's inception through its completion. In particular, editor Meghan Cleary's enthusiasm was infectious.

I would like to thank Marsha DeFilippo, Stephen King's personal assistant, who has been a wonderful resource for me over the years. I try not to bug her too much, but she always has the answers to my questions when I do pose them.

Thanks to Robert Jackson for granting access to his amazing collection, a veritable King museum. My literary agent, Michael Psaltis, is the kind of person every writer wants to have on his side. It's an endless source of encouragement to know that someone else out there has my future as a writer on his radar.

My wife, Mary Anne, is my number one fan, and I'm hers. Always.

I picked up a copy of *'Salem's Lot* in a second-hand bookstore in Halifax, Nova Scotia, in 1979. I can't recall any of the other books I purchased that day, but that little black paperback with the drop of red blood was the beginning of my avid interest in the works of Stephen King. At least once every year since then, I've had the pleasure of reading a new novel from him. I've often said that if he decided to write romance novels, I would still read his books because for me it's all about the characters. Thank you for three decades of entertainment, and I hope there will be many more to come.

ENDNOTES

1. Interview with Mike Farren, *Interview* XVI, no. 2 (1986), 68–70.

2. Interview with Brian Truitt, *USA Weekend*, March 8, 2009.

3. "On Becoming a Brand Name," *Fear Itself*, Tim Underwood and Chuck Miller, editors (Underwood-Miller, 1982), 15–42.

4. Interview with Mark Lawson, broadcast on BBC Four on December 11, 2006.

5. Interview with Mark Lawson, broadcast on BBC Four on December 11, 2006.

6. *On Writing* (Scribner, 2000), 26.

7. *On Writing* (Scribner, 2000), 51.

8. "The Once and Future Stephen King," Jill Owens, powells.com, November 2006. http://www.powells.com/interviews/ stephenking.html, November 15, 2006.

9. *On Writing* (Scribner, 2000), 73.

10. Bill Thompson, "A Girl Named Carrie," *Kingdom of Fear*, Tim Underwood and Chuck Miller, editors (Underwood-Miller, 1986), 29–33.

11. "From Textbook to Checkbook," Robert W. Wells, *Milwaukee Journal*, September 15, 1980. Reprinted in *Feast of Fear*. Tim Underwood and Chuck Miller, editors. (Underwood-Miller, 1986), 6–8.

12. Interview with Charles L. Grant, *Monsterland Magazine*, June 1985, 30.

13. Interview with Charles L. Grant, *Monsterland Magazine*, June 1985, 30.

14. Stephen Spignesi interview with David King, *The Shape Under the Sheet* (Overlook Connection Press, 1991), 31–38.

15. *Walden Book Report* (December 1997).

16. *On Writing* (Scribner, 2000), 87.

17. Bill Thompson, Introduction, *Kingdom of Fear*, Tim Underwood and Chuck Miller, editors (Underwood-Miller, 1986), 29–33.

18. Interview with Stanley Wiater, 1990, http://www.alteredearth.com/ wiater/king.htm, April 4, 2009.

19. Introduction, *'Salem's Lot* (Pocket Books, 1999), xv–xx.

20. "On Becoming a Brand Name," *Fear Itself*, Tim Underwood and Chuck Miller, editors (Underwood Miller, 1982), 15–42.

21. "On Becoming a Brand Name," *Fear Itself*, Tim Underwood and Chuck Miller, editors (Underwood Miller, 1982), 15–42.

22. Introduction, *'Salem's Lot* (Pocket Books, 1999) , xv–xx.

23. "On Becoming a Brand Name," *Fear Itself,* Tim Underwood and Chuck Miller, editors (Underwood Miller, 1982), 15–42.

24. "On Becoming a Brand Name," *Fear Itself,* Tim Underwood and Chuck Miller, editors (Underwood Miller, 1982), 15–42.

25. "On The Shining and Other Perpetrations," *Whispers* 17–18, vol. 5, nos. 1–2 (August 1982), 11–16.

26. "On The Shining and Other Perpetrations," *Whispers* 17–18, vol. 5, nos. 1–2 (August 1982), 11–16.

27. "On The Shining and Other Perpetrations," *Whispers* 17–18, vol. 5, nos. 1–2 (August 1982), 11–16.

28. *On Writing* (Scribner, 2000), 95.

29. *Danse Macabre* (Everest House, 1981), 254.

30. *Playboy* interview, Eric Norden, June 1983, 74.

31. *Danse Macabre* (Everest House, 1981), 253.

32. Introduction to *The Shining* (Pocket Books, 2001), xv–xviii.

33. Introduction to *The Shining* (Pocket Books, 2001) , xv–xviii.

34. Paul Janeczko, "In Their Own Words: An Interview with Stephen King," *English Journal* 69, no. 2 (February 1980), 9–10.

35. *On Writing* (Scribner, 2000), 207.

36. Introduction to *The Shining* (Pocket Books, 2001), xv–xviii.

37. Interview with Michael Kilgore, *Tampa Tribune*, August 31, 1980. Reprinted in *Bare Bones: Conversations on Terror With Stephen King*, Tim Underwood and Chuck Miller, editors (McGraw-Hill, 1988), 101–111.

38. " King's 'Shining' Returning As A Miniseries," Luaine Lee, Knight-Ridder/Tribune News Service, April 20, 1997. http://community. seattletimes.nwsource.com/archive/?date=19970420&slug=2534 728, April 5, 2009.

39. "King of the Thrill," David L. Ulin, *Los Angeles Times*, October 9, 1998, E1.

40. "On Becoming a Brand Name," *Fear Itself*, Tim Underwood and Chuck Miller, editors (Underwood Miller, 1982), 15–42.

41. Introduction to *The Shining* (Pocket Books, 2001), xv–xviii.

42. "On Becoming a Brand Name," *Fear Itself*, Tim Underwood and Chuck Miller, editors (Underwood Miller, 1982), 15–42.

43. *Danse Macabre* (Everest House, 1981), 373.

44. *Danse Macabre* (Everest House, 1981), 371.

45. *On Writing* (Scribner, 2000), 202.

46. "Shine of the Times," Marty Ketchum, Pat Cadigan, and Lewis Shiner. *Shayol* 1, no. 3 (Summer, 1979), 43–46.

47. "Stephen King's God Trip," John Marks, *Salon*, October 23, 2008, http://www.salon.com/books/int/2008/10/23/stephen_king/ April 4, 2009.

48. Preface, *The Stand: Uncut and Expanded Edition* (Doubleday, 1990), ix–xii.

49 Interview with Bhob Stewart, *Heavy Metal* (February 1980), 53.

50 Interview with Richard Wolinsky and Lawrence Davison, KPFA-FM, September 8, 1979. From a transcript in *Feast of Fear*, Tim Underwood and Chuck Miller, editors (Carroll & Graf, 1989), 22–31.

51 "Shine of the Times," Marty Ketchum, Pat Cadigan, and Lewis Shiner. *Shayol* 1, no. 3 (Summer, 1979), 43–46.

52 "The Man Who Writes Nightmares," Mel Allen, *Yankee* 43, no. 3 March 1979, 127–128.

53 Interview with Paul R. Gagne, *Feast of Fear*, Tim Underwood and Chuck Miller, editors (Carroll & Graf, 1989), 90–108.

54 Interview with Michael Kilgore, *Tampa Tribune*, August 31, 1980. Reprinted in *Bare Bones: Conversations on Terror With Stephen King*, Tim Underwood and Chuck Miller, editors (McGraw-Hill, 1988), 101–111.

55 *Danse Macabre* (Everest House, 1981), 371.

56 *On Writing* (Scribner, 2000), 201.

57 *Danse Macabre* (Everest House, 1981), 371–372.

58 *On Writing* (Scribner, 2000), 203.

59 Preface, *The Stand: Uncut and Expanded Edition* (Doubleday, 1990), ix–xii.

60 Preface, *The Stand: Uncut and Expanded Edition* (Doubleday, 1990) , ix–xii.

61 An Evening with Stephen King at the Billerica, Massachusetts Public Library, April 22, 1983.

62 "The Art of Fiction No. 189," The *Paris Review* 178 (Fall 2006), 66–101.

63 Douglas E. Winter, *The Art of Darkness* (NAL, 1984), 76.

64 Douglas E. Winter, *The Art of Darkness* (NAL, 1984), 76.

65 Interview with Paul R. Gagne. *Feast of Fear*, Tim Underwood and Chuck Miller, editors (Carroll & Graf, 1989), 90–108.

66 Interview with Christopher Evans, *Minneapolis Star*, September 8, 1979. Reprinted in *Bare Bones: Conversations on Terror With Stephen King*, Tim Underwood and Chuck Miller, editors (McGraw-Hill, 1988), 90–92.

67 "Stephen King's Court of Horror," Abe Peck, *Rolling Stone College Papers* (Winter 1980). Reprinted in *Bare Bones: Conversations on Terror With Stephen King*, Tim Underwood and Chuck Miller, editors (McGraw-Hill, 1988), 93–101.

68 Interview with Christopher Evans, *Minneapolis Star*, September 8, 1979. Reprinted in *Bare Bones: Conversations on Terror With Stephen King*, Tim Underwood and Chuck Miller, editors (McGraw-Hill, 1988), 90–92.

69 Interview with Paul R. Gagne. *Feast of Fear*, Tim Underwood and Chuck Miller, editors (Carroll & Graf, 1989), 90–108.

70 *On Writing* (Scribner, 2000), 192.

71 "Excavating ID Monsters," Stan Nicholls, *September* 1998. http://www.herebedragons.co.uk/nicholls/interviews.htm, April 5, 2009.

72 *On Writing* (Scribner, 2000), 192.

73 Interview with Michael Kilgore, *Tampa Tribune*, August 31, 1980. Reprinted in *Bare Bones: Conversations on Terror With Stephen King*, Tim Underwood and Chuck Miller, editors (McGraw-Hill, 1988), 101–111.

74 *On Writing* (Scribner, 2000), 169.

75 "Entering the Rock Zone," *Castle Rock* 3, no. 10 (October 1987), 1.

76 Introduction, *Pet Sematary* (Pocket Books, 2001), ix–xiii.

77 Introduction, *Pet Sematary* (Pocket Books, 2001), ix–xiii.

78 Interview with Mike Farren, *Interview* XVI, no. 2 (1986), 68–70.

79 Interview with Richard Wolinsky and Lawrence Davison, KPFA-FM, September 8, 1979. From a transcript in *Feast of Fear*, Tim Underwood and Chuck Miller, editors (Carroll & Graf, 1989), 22–31.

80 "The Wendigo" by Algernon Blackwood. From *The Lost Valley and Other Stories* (Eveleigh Nash, 1910).

81 "Stephen King Comments on *It*," *Castle Rock* 2, no. 7 (July 1986), 1.

82 "How *It* Happened," *Book-of-the-Month Club News* (October, 1986), 3, 5.

83 "Stephen King Comments on *It*," *Castle Rock* 2, no. 7 (July 1986), 1.

84 Douglas E. Winter, *The Art of Darkness*, (NAL, 1984), 153.

85 Interview with Stephen Schaefer, *Boston Herald*, July 27, 1986. Reprinted in *Feast of Fear*. Tim Underwood and Chuck Miller, editors. (Underwood-Miller, 1986), 192–203.

86 Interview with Stephen Schaefer, *Boston Herald*, July 27, 1986. Reprinted in *Feast of Fear*. Tim Underwood and Chuck Miller, editors. (Underwood-Miller, 1986), 192–203.

87 "The Limits of Fear," Jo Fletcher, *Knave* 19, no. 5 (1987). Reprinted in *Feast of Fear*. Tim Underwood and Chuck Miller, editors. (Underwood-Miller, 1986), 258–265.

88 "The King of the Macabre at Home," Michael J. Bandler, *Parents* (January 1982). Reprinted in *Feast of Fear*. Tim Underwood and Chuck Miller, editors. (Underwood-Miller, 1986), 221–226.

89 "The Art of Fiction No. 189," The *Paris Review* 178 (Fall 2006), 66–101.

90 "Stephen King's Court of Horror," Abe Peck, *Rolling Stone College Papers* (Winter 1980). Reprinted in *Bare Bones: Conversations on Terror With Stephen King*, Tim Underwood and Chuck Miller, editors (McGraw-Hill, 1988), 93–101.

91 Naomi Epel, *Writers Dreaming* (Clarkson Potter, 1983), 134–143.

92 FAQ, www.stephenking.com http://www.stephenking.com/faq.html#1.6, April 5, 2009.

93 "Why I Was Bachman," *The Bachman Books* (NAL, 1985), v–x.

94 "Why I Was Bachman," *The Bachman Books* (NAL, 1985), v–x.

95 "An Evening With Stephen King," Secret Windows, (Book-of-the-Month Club, 2000), 387–401.

96 "Stephen King Comments on *It*," *Castle Rock* 2, no. 7 (July 1986), 1.

97 Tony Magistrale, *Stephen King, The Second Decade* (Twayne Publishers, 1992), 13.

98 Tony Magistrale, *Stephen King, The Second Decade* (Twayne Publishers, 1992), 6.

99 Interview with Nigel Farndale, *Sydney Morning Herald*, December 9, 2006.

100 Douglas E. Winter, *The Art of Darkness* (NAL, 1984), 155.

101 *On Writing* (Scribner, 2001), 96.

102 *On Writing* (Scribner, 2001), 96.

103 John Katzenbach, "Sheldon Gets the Ax," *New York Times*, May 31, 1987, Section 7, page 20.

104 Interview with Ed Gorman, *Mystery Scene* 10 (August 1987), 26–29.

105 "Excavating ID Monsters," Stan Nicholls, *September* 1998. http://www.herebedragons.co.uk/nicholls/interviews.htm, April 5, 2009.

106 *On Writing* (Scribner, 2000), 165.

107 *On Writing* (Scribner, 2000), 166.

108 *On Writing* (Scribner, 2000), 168,

109 "Excavating ID Monsters," Stan Nicholls, *September* 1998. http://www.herebedragons.co.uk/nicholls/interviews.htm, April 5, 2009.

110 "Tabitha King, Co-Miser-ating with Stephen King," *Castle Rock* 3, no. 8 (August 1987), 1.

111 "Interview with Stephen King," Lynn Flewelling, SFF.net, August 1990. http://www.sff.net/people/Lynn.Flewelling/s.stephen.king.html, April 5, 2009.

112 Interview with Ed Gorman, *Mystery Scene* 10 (August 1987), 26–29.

113 *On Writing* (Scribner, 2000), 168.

114 "King's Features," interview with David Hochman, *Entertainment Weekly*, July 2, 1999.

115 "The Art of Fiction No. 189," The *Paris Review* 178 (Fall 2006), 66–101.

116 Introduction, *The Green Mile* (Plume, 1997), v–viii.

117 Introduction, *The Green Mile* (Plume, 1997), v–viii.

118 Introduction, *The Green Mile: The Two Dead Girls* (Signet, 1996), vii–xiii.

119 Introduction, *The Green Mile: The Two Dead Girls* (Signet, 1996), vii–xiii.

120 Introduction, *The Green Mile: The Screenplay* (Scribner Paperback Fiction, 1999), ix–xi.

121 America Online Chat, March 1996. Transcript: http://www.stephen-king.de/interviews/aol96.html, April 5, 2009.

122 Introduction, *The Green Mile: The Two Dead Girls* (Signet, 1996), vii–xiii.

123 Introduction, *The Green Mile: The Two Dead Girls* (Signet, 1996), vii–xiii.

124 *On Writing* (Scribner, 2000), 197.

125 "An Evening With Stephen King," Secret Windows, (Book-of-the-Month Club, 2000), 387–401.

126 Introduction to *The Shawshank Redemption: The Shooting Script* (Newmarket Press, 1996), ix–xii.

127 The Book Reporter, November 21, 1997. http://www.teenreads.com/authors/au-king-stephen.asp#pastview, April 5, 2009.

128 "Getting Spooked By King's Tactic," Martin Arnold, *New York Times*, November 5, 1997, E3.

129 "What Are You Afraid Of?" Mark Singer, *New Yorker*, September 7, 1998, 56–67.

130 "Secrets, Lies and *Bag of Bones*," Amazon.com, October 1998, http://www.geocities.com/willemfh/king/mail_king.htm, April 4, 2009.

131 "Love, Death and Stephen King," Amazon.com, 1998, http://www.amazon.com/gp/feature.html?ie=UTF8&docId=5604, April 4, 2009.

132 "Love, Death and Stephen King," Amazon.com, 1998, http://www.amazon.com/gp/feature.html?ie=UTF8&docId=5604, April 4, 2009.

133 "The Art of Fiction No. 189," The *Paris Review* 178 (Fall 2006), 66–101.

134 "News From the Dead Zone," Bev Vincent, *Cemetery Dance* 37 (December 2001),24–25.

135 "Weathering Heights," Michael Rowe, *Fangoria* 18¹ (April 1999), 34–38.

136 "Love, Death and Stephen King," Amazon.com, 1998. http://www.amazon.com/gp/feature.html?ie=UTF8&docId=5604, April 5, 2009.

137 Interview with Andrew O'Hehir, Salon, September 24, 1998, http://www.salon.com/books/int/1998/09/cov_si_24int.html, April 4, 2009.

138 Letter to Readers, Scribner Web site, April 1998. http://www.simonsays.com/king, April 15, 1998.

139 Interview with Joyce Lynch Dewes Moore, *Mystery* (March 1981). Reprinted in *Bare Bones: Conversations on Terror with Stephen King*, Tim Underwood and Chuck Miller, editors (McGraw-Hill, 1988), 68–76.

140 *On Writing* (Scribner, 2000), 253.

141 *On Writing* (Scribner, 2000), 254.

142 *On Writing* (Scribner, 2000), 256.

143 "A sad face behind the scary mask," Nigel Farndale, *The Sunday Telegraph*, November 25, 2006. http://www.theage.com.au/news/books/a-sad-face-behind-the-scary-mask/2006/11/23/1163871548220.html, November 28, 2006.

144 *On Writing* (Scribner, 2000), 267.

145 Interview with Kim Murphy, *Los Angeles Times*, January 27, 2002, F-3.

146 Chris Nashawaty, "Stephen King Quits," *Entertainment Weekly*, September 27, 2002.

147 Author's Note, *Dreamcatcher* (Scribner, 2001), 619–620.

148 Interview with Paula Zahn, CNN, October 31, 2003. Transcript: http://transcripts.cnn.com/TRANSCRIPTS/0310/31/pzn.00.html, April 5, 2009.

149 "The Politics of Limited Editions," part 1, *Castle Rock* 1, no. 6 (June 1985), 3.

150 Introduction, *The Green Mile: The Two Dead Girls* (Signet, March 1996), vii–xiii.

151 Afterword, *The Waste Lands* (Donald M. Grant, 1992), 511–512.

152 Peter Straub, interview with Jeff Zaleski, *Publishers Weekly*, August 20, 2001. http://www.publishersweekly.com/article/CA152899.html April 5, 2009.

153 Interview with Ben Reese, Amazon.com, May 2003. http://www.amazon.com/gp/feature.html?ie=UTF8&docId=455676, April 4, 2009.

154 Chris Nashawaty, "Stephen King Quits," *Entertainment Weekly*, September 27, 2002.

155 Interview with Kim Murphy, *Los Angeles Times*, January 27, 2002, F-3.

156 Chris Nashawaty, "Stephen King Quits," *Entertainment Weekly*, September 27, 2002.

157 Afterword, *Wizard and Glass* (Donald M. Grant, 1997), 785–787.

158 Afterword, *The Dark Tower VII: The Dark Tower* (Scribner, 2004), 861–863.

159 *Ubris*, 1969, and *Moth*, 1970; *The Devil's Wine*, Tom Piccirilli, editor (Cemetery Dance Publications, 2004).

160 *Walden Book Report* (July 2003).

161 *Everything's Eventual* (Scribner, 2002), 70.

162 Interview with Paula Zahn, CNN, October 31, 2003. Transcript: http://transcripts.cnn.com/TRANSCRIPTS/0310/31/pzn.00.html, April 5, 2009.

163 Stephen King, National Book Award Ceremony acceptance speech, November 19, 2003.

164 Stephen King, National Book Award Ceremony acceptance speech, November 19, 2003.

165 "The Once and Future Stephen King," Jill Owens, powells.com, November 2006. http://www.powells.com/interviews/stephenking.html, November 15, 2006.

166 Interview with Hans-Åke Lilja, Lilja's Library, January 17, 2007, http://www.liljas-library.com/showinterview.php?id=35, April 4, 2009.

167 "How Lisey Found Her Story," Ben P. Indick, *Publishers Weekly*, August 28, 2006. http://www.publishersweekly.com/article/CA6365987.html, April 5, 2009.

168 Interview with Mark Lawson, broadcast on BBC Four on December 11, 2006.

169 "The Once and Future Stephen King," Jill Owens, powells.com, November 2006. http://www.powells.com/interviews/stephenking.html, November 15, 2006.

170 Afterword, *Lisey's Story* (Scribner, 2006), 511–512.

171 "A sad face behind the scary mask," Nigel Farndale, The *Sunday Telegraph*, November 25, 2006. http://www.theage.com.au/news/books/a-sad-face-behind-the-scary-mask/2006/11/23/1163871548220.html, November 28, 2006.

172 David Fite, *Harold Bloom: The Rhetoric of Romantic Vision* (University of Massachusetts Press, 1985), 221.

173 Harold Bloom, Introduction to *Stephen King: Modern Critical Views* (Chelsea House, 1998), 1–3.

174 Harold Bloom, "For the World of Letters, It's a Horror," *Los Angeles Times*, September 19, 2003, B-13.

175 Interview with Paula Zahn, CNN, October 31, 2003. Transcript: http://transcripts.cnn.com/TRANSCRIPTS/0310/31/pzn.00.html, April 5, 2009.

176 "Who's Afraid of the Dark?" Matt Thorne, *London Independent*, November 12, 2006. http://www.independent.co.uk/arts-entertainment/books/features/stephen-king-whos-afraid-of-the-dark-424024.html, April 5, 2009.

177 "A sad face behind the scary mask," Nigel Farndale, The *Sunday Telegraph*, November 25, 2006. http://www.theage.com.au/news/books/a-sad-face-behind-the-scary-mask/2006/11/23/1163871548220.html, November 28, 2006.

178 Message board post, www.stephenking.com, June 2008, http://www.stephenking.com/forums/showthread.php?t=7519, April 4, 2009.

179 "Stephen King's God Trip," John Marks, Salon, October 23, 2008, http://www.salon.com/books/int/2008/10/23/stephen_king/ April 4, 2009.

180 Interview with Hans-Åke Lilja, Lilja's Library, January 18, 2007, http://www.liljas-library.com/showinterview.php?id=36, April 4, 2009.

IMAGE CREDITS

Every effort has been made to trace copyright holders. If any unintended omissions have been made, becker&mayer! would be pleased to add appropriate acknowledgments in future editions.

Front cover: Photo by Amy Guip

Page 7: Susan Aimee Weinik/Time & Life Pictures/Getty Images

Page 8: Courtesy of Stephen King

Page 9: Photo by Amy Guip

Page 11: Courtesy of Stephen King

Page 12: Courtesy of Stephen King

Page 13: Courtesy of Stephen King

Page 14: Courtesy of Stephen King

Page 15: Courtesy of Stephen King (photo); Courtesy of Bob Jackson (inserts)

Page 16: Courtesy of Stephen King

Page 17: Courtesy of Stephen King

Page 18: Courtesy of Stephen King; Photo by David King (bottom)

Page 19: Courtesy of Bob Jackson

Page 20: Courtesy of Bob Jackson (all)

Page 21: Courtesy of Bob Jackson; Photo strip courtesy of Stephen King

Page 22: Courtesy of Bob Jackson

Page 23: Photo by Frank Kadi/Courtesy of Bob Jackson

Page 25: Courtesy of Stephen King/Fogler Library

Page 26: Courtesy of Doubleday Publishing Group

Page 28: Courtesy of Bob Jackson

Page 29: Courtesy of Bob Jackson

Page 30: Courtesy of Stephen King/Fogler Library

Page 31: Courtesy of Stephen King

Page 32: The Everett Collection

Page 33: Courtesy of Bob Jackson

Page 35: Courtesy of Doubleday Publishing Group

Page 36: Alex Gotfryd/CORBIS

Page 37: The Everett Collection

Page 38: Courtesy of Stephen King

Page 39: Courtesy of Stephen King/Fogler Library

Page 40: Courtesy of Bob Jackson

Page 41: Courtesy of Stephen King/Fogler Library (inserts)

Page 42: Courtesy of Katherine Flickinger

Page 43: Courtesy of Katherine Flickinger

Page 44: Courtesy of Katherine Flickinger

Page 45: Courtesy of Stephen King/Fogler Library

Page 47: Courtesy of Bob Jackson

Page 48: Courtesy of Stephen King/Fogler Library

Page 49: Courtesy of Stephen King

Page 50: Duel with Clubs (oil on canvas), Goya y Lucientes, Francisco Jose de (1746-1828) / Prado, Madrid, Spain / Lauros / Giraudon / The Bridgeman Art Library

Page 51: Courtesy of Doubleday Publishing Group

Page 52: AP Photo

Page 55: Courtesy of Stephen King/Fogler Library

Page 56: The Everett Collection

Page 58: Courtesy of Stephen King

Page 59: Courtesy of Stephen King/Fogler Library (inserts)

Page 60: Courtesy of Bob Jackson

Page 61: Courtesy of Tom Jones/Life Magazine

Page 62: Courtesy of The Penguin Group

Page 63: Courtesy of Stephen King

Page 64: Courtesy of Stephen King

Page 65: The Everett Collection

Page 66: Courtesy of Stephen King

Page 67: Courtesy of Stephen King

Page 68: Courtesy of Stephen King

Page 69: Courtesy of Stephen King

Page 70: Courtesy of Futura Publications, UK

Page 71: Courtesy of Tom Jones/Life Magazine (photo); Courtesy of Stephen King/Fogler Library (inserts)

Page 73: Courtesy of De Laurentiis Entertainment Group

Page 74: Courtesy of Mark Molea (via Flickr.com)

Page 75: Courtesy of Jim Leonard

Page 76: Courtesy of Jamie Cole (www.jamie-cole.com)

Page 77: The Everett Collection

Page 79: Courtesy of Thomas Victor

Page 80: The Everett Collection

Page 82: Courtesy of Doubleday Publishing Group

Page 83: Courtesy of Stephen King/Fogler Library (insert)

Page 85: Rex USA

Page 86: Courtesy of Kristborg Whitney (via Flickr.com)

Page 87: Courtesy of Stephen King

Page 88: Stratford Library Association, Stratford, Connecticut, USA

Page 89: Courtesy of Emily Qualey (via Flickr.com)

Page 90: Courtesy of New American Library

Page 91: Courtesy of Stephen King/Fogler Library

Page 92: Courtesy of Paul Davis (via Flickr.com)

Page 94: Courtesy of The Penguin Group

Page 95: Courtesy of Stephen King/Fogler Library (insert)

Page 96: Courtesy of Stephen King/Fogler Library

Page 97: Courtesy of Stephen King/Fogler Library

Page 98: Jose Azel/Aurora/Getty Images

Page 100: Courtesy of Jim Leonard

Page 101: The Everett Collection; Courtesy of Stephen King (insert)

Page 102: Courtesy of The Penguin Group

Page 103: Courtesy of The Penguin Group

Page 105: Courtesy of Andrew Unangst

Page 106: The Everett Collection

Page 107: Courtesy of Stephen King/Fogler Library

Page 108: Unknown

Page 109: Courtesy of Luis Ramos

Page 110: Courtesy of Bob Jackson

Page 111: Courtesy of The Penguin Group

Page 112: Courtesy of Warner Bros. Entertainment, Inc.

Page 113: The Kobal Collection

Page 114: The Kobal Collection

Page 115: AP Photo

Page 117: AP Photo

Page 118: Courtesy of Natiya Guin

Page 119: Courtesy of Stephen King/Fogler Library

Page 121: Courtesy of Stephen King

Page 122: Illustration by Ray Russotto

Page 123: Courtesy of Scribner Book Company

Page 124: Courtesy of Stephen King/Fogler Library

Page 125: Courtesy of Stephen King/Fogler Library

Page 126: CORBIS SYGMA

Page 127: Courtesy of Stephen King

Page 128: Courtesy of Stephen King

Page 129: Margaret Norton/NBCU Photo Bank via AP Images

Page 130: Courtesy of Audrey Sparks

Page 131: AP Photo/Robert F. Bukaty

Page 133: Courtesy of Scribner Book Company

Page 134: Rex Rystedt/Time & Life Pictures/Getty Images

Page 135: Carl D. Walsh / Aurora Photos

Page 136: Mitchell Gerber/CORBIS

Page 137: Courtesy of Time Inc.

Page 138: Courtesy of Motion Picture Corporation of America

Page 140: Courtesy of Stephen King/Fogler Library

Page 141: Photo by David King

Page 142: Courtesy of Stephen King/Fogler Library

Page 143: Courtesy of Jill Krementz

Page 144: Courtesy of Michael Whelan

Page 145: Courtesy of Jim Leonard

Page 146: Courtesy of Jim Leonard

Page 147: Courtesy of Stephen King/Fogler Library (inserts)

Page 149: Courtesy of Stephen King

Page 150: Courtesy of The Penguin Group

Page 151: Courtesy of Bob Jackson

Page 153: AP Photo/CP, Aaron Harris

Page 154: Rex USA

Page 156: Matthew Peyton/Getty Images for MWA

Page 158: Courtesy of Bob Jackson

Page 159: Courtesy of Scribner Book Compan

Page 160: Bertrand Langlois/AFP/Getty Images

Page 161: Mario Tama/Getty Images

Page 162: Rich Pilling/MLB Photos via Getty Images

Page 163: AP Photo/Chris O'Meara

Page 165: Courtesy of Thomas R. Hindman/Bangor Daily News

Page 166: Photo by Chris Campbell

Page 167: Photos by Chris Campbell

Page 169: Photo by Amy Guip